Blessings *from the* Fall

Turning a Fall from Grace into a New Beginning

BEVERLY ENGEL

Health Communications, Inc.
Deerfield Beach, Florida

www.hci-online.com

Library of Congress Cataloging-in-Publication Data

Engel, Beverly.
    Blessings from the fall: turning a fall from grace into a new
  beginning / Beverly Engel.
        p.   cm.
    ISBN 1-55874-456-8 (trade paper)
    1. Failure (Psychology) 2. Loss (Psychology) I. Title.
BF575.F14E54 1997   96-39728
155.9—dc21   CIP

Publisher: Health Communications, Inc.
            3201 S.W. 15th Street
            Deerfield Beach, Florida 33442-8190

Cover photo ©1996 PhotoDisc, Inc.
Cover design by Lawna Patterson Oldfield

Contents

Part III: Blessings from the Fall

Part IV: Rising from Your Fall

Part V: When a Loved One Falls from Grace

Acknowledgments

First and foremost, I wish to thank and acknowledge my dear friends Sharon Kwast and Patti McDermott, who supported me through my personal fall from grace. Their encouragement and non-judgmental stance helped me to survive my fall and then to rise out of the ashes to become a new version of myself. My wish is that everyone who experiences a fall could be blessed with such friends.

I also wish to express my deep appreciation for Barbara Stephens, the fine Jungian analyst who was there for me in my darkest days, willing to hear my darkest secrets without judgment and to help me acknowledge and finally accept my dark side. With her help I learned to appreciate my Shadow, to allow it to fill up my empty places and fill out my personality.

I am also grateful for my generous friend, Lucia Capacchione, who connected me with Health Communications and who has been supportive of this book all along.

A special thanks to Michele Pillar Carlton, Richard Berendzen, Dannion Brinkley and all the others who so bravely told their stories so others could learn from their fall.

And last but not least, I wish to thank the staff at Health Communications: Peter Vegso, Matthew Diener, Mark Colucci and Kim Weiss.

Introduction

Have you come to the Red Sea place in your life
Where, in spite of all you can do,
There is no way out, there is no way back,
There is no other way but through?

ANNIE JOHNSON FLINT

M y own fall came as a result of a buildup of situations and emotions that had been brewing for several years. I was just turning 40, in an emotionally intense but stifling relationship, and burnt out after working for more than 10 years with survivors of childhood sexual abuse. New memories of my own neglectful, abusive childhood were surfacing more and more, and I was estranged from my mother. I had just completed my first book, *The Right to Innocence: Healing the Trauma of Childhood Sexual*

Abuse, and by so doing had accomplished a lifelong dream of writing a book.

I suddenly felt stymied by my life. I wanted freedom: from my relationship, from my practice, from being a responsible adult. Like many who experience a mid-life crisis, I had fantasies of changing my life entirely—having several wild love affairs, moving away, becoming a full-time writer. I couldn't believe time had swept by so quickly. "How could I be turning 40?" I'd ask myself in amazement. I didn't feel 40. Inside I felt much younger and I wanted to *live.* I wanted to grab all the passion that life still had in store for me.

But I loved my partner, I was dedicated to my clients, and I needed to support myself. I couldn't go off on some tangent. The responsible part of me wouldn't let me.

And so I kept right on with my practice and tried again to make my relationship work. I focused on editing my book and let myself get carried away with fantasies of it becoming a bestseller.

For years I had dedicated myself to helping and pleasing others, and being the best person I could possibly be. But like so many others who try to be "all good," I had stored up quite a few dark feelings and desires. I was discovering more and more that I wasn't going to be able to control that hidden dark side of myself for much longer. Much to my chagrin, it began to seep out every now and then—just enough to keep me off-balance. I went out with friends to celebrate the sale of my book to a publisher, drank too much, said horrible things to a good friend, and risked my life and that of a friend (and God knows who else) by driving drunk.

This scared me sufficiently to cut down on my drinking, give up my fantasies of starting a new life and settle back into my so-called normal one. Or so I thought.

And then I "fell in love." I put quotes around the phrase because what I experienced had nothing to do with love. It had everything to do with the fact that I needed to get out of my relationship and didn't know how. It had everything to do with the fact that I wasn't speaking to my mother. It had everything to do with some unresolved issues from a previous experience in my own therapy that were crying out to be dealt with. And it had everything to do with the fact that I'd been hiding behind the persona of "therapist" for too long.

Naturally, the person I fell in love with was someone who was forbidden, someone who saw me as a "savior," someone I could hide with once more. I lied to my partner and broke my partner's heart. I destroyed the trust of someone who had never trusted anyone before.

Of course, the new relationship was a disaster, one that severely damaged us both emotionally. Once again I decided I needed to get away. I bought a vacation home in a small town I'd always loved and started going there by myself. I made plans to move there in a year. I began therapy once again. Things started looking up.

During the writing of my third book, *The Emotionally Abused Woman,* I had a breakthrough. As I wrote about the emotionally abusive partner, boss and parent, I was suddenly struck by the awareness that I fit the description of an abusive person. To say that I was shocked by this revelation would be an understatement. I had always seen myself as the victim in relationships, the one who was neglected, emotionally abused, misunderstood. Now I was faced with the painful truth: I had also done my share of abusing. And horror upon horrors, I recognized how much like my emotionally abusive mother I had become. I was just as critical and judgmental as she, just as demanding, and just as verbally abusive, particularly when I was drinking.

Then the worst two years of my life began. I recognized I was also just as narcissistic as my mother. A dog I adored was stolen from me, and I was surprised by how crushed I was over it. My mother died a long, painful death a few months after we had finally reconciled. The bottom fell out of the real estate market and I couldn't sell my house in Los Angeles, nor my mother's house in Bakersfield. Now I had three mortgages and I'd already told everyone I was leaving Los Angeles in a year, so I wasn't getting any new clients. And I'd already leased a building in the new area for a new center. I was going down fast.

I ended up losing nearly everything I'd worked for years to build up. I couldn't continue paying for the lease on my new office space because the center I'd started wasn't going so well. Suddenly people were once again doubting the word of sexual abuse victims, partly due to the power of the False Memory Society, which claimed that therapists were brainwashing their clients into believing that certain events had taken place when they had not. Sexual abuse survivors were having a difficult time trusting therapists and weren't seeking help the way they once had. By the time I closed my offices in L.A., I was nearly broke.

All I had left was my writing. Then an article appeared in the *New York Times* accusing me, along with several other "recovery" writers, of starting a "witch-hunt" and convincing clients they had been sexually abused when they had not. Now my reputation was in question as well. On top of everything else, the "recovery" market suddenly dried up. Publishers were no longer buying books about addiction/recovery issues, which was my specialty and the area on which I had built my reputation. The market had become so saturated that my next two book proposals were turned down.

I'd become so well known as a writer of books on recovery issues that I was having a difficult time breaking into a new market. I couldn't sell a book and I had hardly any money left. I was in a new town, away from all my friends, away from my clients. I was no longer working as a therapist and I did not have a book contract. I was either going to sink or swim. I had to find out what I was made of. I did.

That is what this book is all about: Finding out what you are really made of. Looking deep into yourself and discovering who you *really* are. Discovering the blessings that inevitably come from a fall from grace.

Although at times I am brutally honest in this book, sometimes confronting you with information or challenging you to reach inside yourself and become more honest about your role in your fall, I want you to know that I have, in fact, walked in your shoes and have nothing but empathy for your pain, your grief and your shame.

I can relate to every one of the examples I have presented in the book. Like Jack, I had a drinking problem and often drove while intoxicated. It was only for the grace of God that I did not cause an accident that maimed or killed other people. Like Max and Melody, I too have narcissistic tendencies, and, like Marion, I became so involved in working with my clients that I neglected the work that needed to be done on myself.

By sharing with you parts of my story throughout the book and allowing you to see inside me, I hope to inspire you to be as honest with yourself and as vulnerable. The time for hiding is over. Your covers have already been pulled off. Now it's time to reveal yourself to yourself.

PART I

AFTER THE FALL

Falling from Grace

It was all happening in a great,
swooping free-fall, irreversible, free of decision,
in the full pull of gravity toward
whatever was to be.

LAURA Z. HOBSON

If you have made mistakes . . .
there is always another chance for you . . .
you may have a fresh start any moment you choose,
for this thing we call "failure" is not the falling
down, but the staying down.

MARY PICKFORD

There are few experiences in life as demoralizing, humiliating and painful as falling from grace. For some, falling from grace is the horrible, shame-inducing experience of being publicly chastised or humiliated, having their reputation ruined, their good name irretrievably damaged and being robbed of their dignity. For others, it is falling off their pedestal after years of being admired, adored and emulated, or losing all they've worked for years to achieve—their financial status, their reputation, their very livelihood.

If you are reading this book, it may be because you have experienced firsthand this shame and/or disgrace, either personally or vicariously through a loved one. If so, you know the horrible all-pervasive shame that follows your every move, every minute of the day; the anguish of having your family humiliated; and the fear that more people will find out about it.

By its very definition, a fall from grace is usually caused by an error in judgment, a lack of impulse control or a misuse of power. But it can also include all those who have experienced a financial crisis and now must adjust to a different lifestyle; those who were once famous for their looks, physical power or celebrity but are no longer in favor; and those who have lost status due to a divorce. In short, a fall from grace is any situation that impacts people's lives in such a manner as to cause them to feel lowered in their own eyes and the eyes of others.

Blessings from the Fall is written for and about people who basically have good intentions and a good heart, ethical people who, much to their own shock and dismay, either break their own moral code of behavior, betray everything they stand for, disappoint those who have trusted them, or deeply hurt another human being. This book is for the dedicated mother who vowed never to abuse her children but in a fit of rage sends her child to the hospital; for the successful woman or man who is involved in an accident while driving drunk and seriously injures or kills the driver of the other vehicle; for the man or woman who risks everything—family and home, career—for an illicit affair.

It is also for and about people who devote their lives to helping others, or to the advancement of an ideal or a cause, but who, through careless action, jeopardize their reputations: the psychologist who becomes sexually involved with a patient; the alcoholic doctor who becomes careless and permanently disables a patient; the priest who sexually abuses a child.

Blessings from the Fall is also for those who have been hurt by such lapses: the wives of every husband discovered to be a philanderer, rapist or child molester; the parents and relatives of a child, grandchild or sibling who has been accused or convicted of a serious crime; the students of every popular teacher accused of sexual abuse or sexual harassment; the wife and congregation of every minister found to be "carrying on" with other women; every business owner who discovers a long-time, trusted employee embezzling funds—in short, everyone whose trust in someone important in his or her life has been shattered. All these people, the fallen and those affected by their fall, have lessons they can learn from the experience.

Last but not least, this book is also intended for psychotherapists, ministers, priests, social workers and health-care providers who work with those who have fallen and with their loved ones.

One Among Many

Unlike those who experience a trauma such as a major illness or accident, a person who falls from grace usually does not get the same kind of support and understanding from loved ones and the community. Because secrecy and shame are involved in most falls, you may find it difficult if not impossible to reach out to others. And although you are experiencing tremendous feelings of loss and grief, unlike those who experience the loss of a loved one, you probably haven't had much acknowledgment of that loss from others—particularly a public acknowledgment.

Although you probably feel more alone than you ever have in your entire life, the truth is you are not alone. There are thousands of others who are suffering the same humiliation and pain. Whether you have been dishonored or discredited because of scandal, bankruptcy, being fired or demoted from a job, or because you are no longer as young, beautiful or famous as you once were, you will find through reading this book that others have experienced similar feelings and have probably reacted in much the same ways that you have.

Among those you will meet: Andrea, a social worker who was fired from her job after an investigation following the death of a small boy on her caseload; Lili, a wealthy, middle-aged socialite who became involved with the wrong man; Melody, an aging beauty who was having a difficult time facing the fact that she was getting older. You'll also meet: Jim, a real-life Dr. Jekyll and Mr. Hyde—a loving husband and father one minute and a careless and angry philanderer the next; Marion, a psychologist who broke her code of ethics to become involved with a client; Adam, a surgeon accused of sexual harassment; Father Murphy, a priest who sexually abused a young boy in his parish; and Jack, who seriously injured two people in a traffic accident he caused while driving intoxicated.

These stories are real, although in most cases the names and other identifying details have been changed to protect the individuals' privacy. Many of these people were clients of mine who sought help after their fall. Some are friends and acquaintances who, after hearing I was writing this book, agreed to have their story told.

Some, like Michele Pillar Carlton, are famous people who had the courage to share their stories and allow me to use their real names. Some are highly publicized cases, like that of former American University president Richard Berendzen, who wrote his own story in his book, *Come Here*. All are people who want you to benefit from their experience.

Whether you are just now sticking your head up from the rubble of your personal collapse, well on your way to recovering from this trauma, or looking back on your fall from grace with the clearer perspective of someone who has weathered the storm and survived, *Blessings from the Fall* will be of benefit to you.

Types of Falls

Richard Nixon, O. J. Simpson, Mike Tyson, Richard Berendzen, Michael Jackson, Bob Packwood, Hugh Grant, Vanessa Williams, Marion Barry and Pete Rose all have something in common. They all experienced a fall from grace: the humiliation, shame and degradation of falling from their position in life to one far less prestigious because of something they did or were accused of doing. I call this a *moral* fall.

There are also less famous and less infamous people who have experienced the same plight. Many people have experienced a moral fall in one way or another— whether it was from having an affair and losing their spouse; from hitting bottom with their alcohol, drug, eating, gambling or sex addiction; or from going against their moral code in some way.

In addition to the moral fall, there are many other types of falls, including:

- *A financial fall*—bankruptcy, foreclosure, loss of a business
- *A legal fall*—being sued, being arrested
- *A career fall*—being passed over or fired, losing an important account or case
- *A relationship fall*—divorce, losing a child custody battle
- *An emotional or psychological fall*—onset of aging, loss of beauty, confrontation by family concerning an addiction, admittance to a detox center, having a nervous breakdown

- *A social fall*—loss of status or celebrity (i.e., being asked to resign from a social club) caused by being involved in a scandal, a divorce, etc.
- *A medical fall*—serious illness or major accident, chronic illness or pain, being accident-prone, extreme lack of energy, extreme weight gain or weight loss

The Positive, Transformative Powers of a Fall

Although I'm sure it is hard to believe, good *can* come out of this seemingly bad situation. In fact, positive transformation can occur. In this book we are going to focus on the positive, transformative powers of such a fall: how a personal crisis of the soul can cause people to reevaluate, restructure and reinvent themselves. Throughout the book I will encourage you to perceive your fall from grace as an opportunity to learn about yourself in profound ways—to literally transform yourself into a better, healthier, fuller human being capable of becoming far more loving and compassionate toward others and yourself.

In the process, I will help you to learn to cope with the reality and consequences of your fall. Instead of yielding to the temptation to run away and hide in shame, you will learn what it takes to face things head on, first in order to discover why you've gotten yourself into this predicament, and then to face those you have hurt along the way.

As you follow Andrea, Lili, Max and others through their transformation from shame and denial to recognition

and self-awareness, and finally to acceptance and gratitude, you will begin to understand how powerful and
life-changing a fall from grace can be. Sometimes you
will see yourself in these stories, other times you may say
to yourself, "At least I didn't do *that*," or "There but for
the grace of God go I." At all times, I hope you will recognize that this book was written for you.

You can allow your fall from grace to destroy you and
your family or you can use it as the catalyst for achieving a whole new life. It is up to you.

What you need now more than anything else is hope.
Hope that things will get better, hope for the future, hope
for a second chance. Hope is often what separates those
who rise from their fall from those who never get up.

Reading about the blessings that others experienced as
a result of their fall can give you that hope. Just knowing
that others survived their fall and actually emerged from
the situation a better person should encourage you to
persevere.

Coping with Your Humiliation, Shame, Anger and Depression

And what looks dark in the distance
may brighten as I draw near.

MARY GARDNER BRAINARD

Hope is the feeling you have that the
feeling you have isn't permanent.

JEAN KERR

Before you can experience the blessings of your fall, you must first get through it. The shame and humiliation that most people suffer as a result of their fall can be so powerful that they are at risk of illness, an emotional breakdown or severe depression.

People have been known to do drastic things when their reputations are ruined, or when they are in danger of losing everything they've worked hard for. Some decide to run away and try to leave it all behind, while others consider suicide.

But you don't need to take such drastic measures. Instead, you need to view your fall as a valuable learning experience that will change your life for the better if you can stick around long enough to learn it. While you may not know what the lesson is at this point, you need to trust that there is one. More than anything else, this will help you to get through the initial humiliation, pain and fear.

Even though you may not think you can do it, you need to get up every morning, put one foot in front of the other and face what is ahead of you. And you must believe that it will get better. Because I promise you, it will. You can't envision it now, I know. That's why I ask you to trust me. Remember, I've been where you are. I know how you are feeling. I've done it and so can you.

More important, trust yourself. Trusting yourself will no doubt be difficult because it may have been your actions or misjudgment that got you into your present predicament. But you've also gotten yourself out of jams before and you will again. Only this time you're going to do it right—with honor, dignity and integrity.

Trusting God (or whatever higher power you believe in) may be even more difficult. You may feel that your creator has forsaken you, or at the very least not answered your prayers for help. But if you can hang in there, you will discover that your fall from grace is a blessing in disguise.

Some feel that their fall is a punishment from God, a way of "cutting them down to size." But I do not believe in a vengeful God. From my own experience and my observations of those I write about in this book, I have come to the conclusion that a fall from grace is a gift from God rather than a reproach.

Throughout the book you will see how others came to realize that their fall was, in fact, a message from God. Some experienced their fall as God's way of getting their attention, while others interpreted the experience as God's way of preparing them for something far more important in their life.

If you've ever believed in a higher power, this is the time to call on that higher power to help you through your fall and to trust in that higher power to do just that. Remind yourself that you are part of a consciousness far more advanced than you can comprehend, that you are a small part of a gigantic force. Trust that God or the universe ultimately has your best interest at heart. This trust will be a necessary part of getting through your fall successfully.

Dealing with Your Guilt and Shame

A fall from grace can create tremendous feelings of guilt and shame. In order to avoid having these strong emotions overpower you, you will need to learn positive ways of

coping with them. One such way is in learning to understand these two often-confused human emotions.

What is the difference between guilt and shame? When
we experience guilt, we may fear punishment, but when
we are punished or have made amends, the guilt is
resolved. When we experience shame, we fear abandonment. In her book *Shame and Guilt,* Jane Middelton-Moz
explains the difference between the two:

> When we experience guilt, we blame our behavior.
> When we experience shame, we blame our character and
> being.
>
> Guilt is associated with wrongdoing. When we feel
> guilty, we feel that we owe a debt to another. Shame is
> associated with wrong-being or a feeling of inferiority
> and worthlessness. [1]

In theory, then, we feel guilty for what we *do* and we
feel shame for what we *are.* But in reality, the feelings of
guilt and shame overlap. We do tend to feel guilty if we
do something we consider to be wrong, but we can also
feel shame for being the kind of person to do such a thing.

The shame caused by a fall from grace is usually powerful enough to change a person forever. This transformation can be positive or negative, depending on how
one perceives and copes with the experience.

The emotion of shame causes us to feel suddenly overwhelmed and self-conscious, so much so that we often

---

[1] Jane Middleton-Moz, *Shame and Guilt: Masters of Disguise* (Deerfield Beach, Fla.:
Health Communications, Inc., 1990), 56.

want to hide from what we experience as the critical eyes of others. We feel exposed and overly visible.

If you allow it to, shame can eat at your spirit in a devastating way. It can cause you to doubt yourself, question your achievements and have misgivings about your relationships. The shame that comes with a fall can be so pervasive that you lose your motivation to continue striving or even to go on with your life. Depression, alcoholism, extreme weight gain or loss, permanent withdrawal from society and suicide attempts are common reactions to a fall from grace if it is not dealt with in the right way.

We are told that shame is the painful feeling of being a flawed human being and that therefore it is an unhealthy emotion. But this isn't necessarily true. First of all, all emotions are natural and therefore healthy, and second, shame can be a message that we are failing to be who we were meant to be. Shame can therefore be the first hope of healing. In other words, as noted author, counselor and teacher Lewis B. Smedes stated in his book, *Shame and Grace,* "If we feel like flawed persons, it may be because we are in fact flawed." [2]

Shame can expose us to parts of ourselves that we have not recognized before and to parts of ourselves we have been reluctant to acknowledge. In this way, it can help us to know ourselves on a very deep level.

There are two kinds of shame, healthy shame and unhealthy shame. According to Smedes, healthy shame is a reminder that we are less than we ought to be and less

---

[2] Lewis B. Smedes, *Shame and Grace: Healing the Shame We Don't Deserve* (San Francisco: HarperSanFrancisco, 1993), 31.

than we want to be. If we can still feel shame, it is because we are healthy enough to feel uncomfortable about this fact.

Those who feel shame for their less-than-noble natures should feel grateful that they still have the power to feel it. As Smedes tells us:

> We are closest to health when we let ourselves feel the pain of our shame and be led by the pain to do something about it.
>
> If I never feel shame, I have become either totally divine or totally corrupt—and my best intuitions tell me I am neither. [3]

Shame does in fact keep us in touch with our better or true self. Smedes goes so far as to say that shame is a gift because it calls us back to our better self. Sometimes it is our conscience that calls us back to our better self. Sometimes it is the stories of those who went before us, from the experienced and the wise. Sometimes it is in the form of a fall from grace.

One of the truest blessings of a fall is that it can cause us to feel healthy shame, and this shame can pull us back from the clutches of our less-than-better selves. When it comes down to it, it is not the threat of punishment or the wrath of God that keeps us true to ourselves. Most of us do the right thing because we would be ashamed of ourselves if we did the wrong thing.

By probing our shame we may discover a great deal about ourselves. What we discover may disappoint us,

---

[3] Smedes, 35.

but it can also give us the gift of self-understanding. It can also cause us to feel grateful for and give ourselves credit for our good qualities. "Whatever there is to discover about ourselves, shame may be the push we need to make us look and see," as Smedes so aptly puts it. [4]

On the other hand, unhealthy shame, or false shame, has no basis in reality. It is false because, unlike true shame, it is not a signal that something is wrong with us. It is unhealthy because it kills our joy and saps our energy and creative powers. Smedes explained it this way: "It is a shame we do not deserve because we are not as bad as our feelings tell us we are." [5]

Even though unhealthy shame is a shame we do not deserve to feel, it is difficult to distinguish it from healthy shame. It may feel the same. In fact, most of us feel both forms of shame from time to time and can even feel both at once. But there are some differences. According to Smedes, unhealthy or false shame:

- Causes us to be unable to distinguish between minor mistakes and major offenses. Every trivial failing feels to us like a crime or sin.
- Causes us to be shame-bound. Nearly anything can bring on a shame attack—a mild criticism, a memory of a past mistake, the suspicion that we are being ignored or mocked by others.
- Is put on us by others. False shame comes from outside of us: from being abused, neglected or

---

[4] Smedes, 36.
[5] Ibid., 37.

controlled by unaccepting parents; from unforgiving, noncompassionate churches and church people; and from a culture that shames us if we are not attractive, rich or smart enough.

- Is indiscriminate and all-pervasive. Unlike healthy shame that zeros in on the problem area, unhealthy shame has no focus. It leaves us feeling like total failures.

Dealing with the Judgments of Others

We live in a very judgmental society. Both those you have hurt and those who hear about your fall will likely be quick to judge and slow to forgive. Therefore, you will need to be prepared for malicious gossip, rejection, or even shunning.

This is what one of my clients shared with me about her experience:

> I'll never forget the first time I went out in public after the scandal. Whenever someone recognized me, they either looked me up and down like I was some kind of freak, or they stared at me in contempt. I was mortified. I wanted to curl up in a little ball and disappear. I couldn't get home fast enough and it was a long time before I showed my face in town again.

The judgments of others can be the worst part of your fall. It is likely that your reputation has meant everything to you. In fact, you may have received the majority of your self-esteem from the adoration and respect of others or from the knowledge that you were doing something positive. That adoration may have been the very impetus that caused you to continually strive for success or the motivator that kept you struggling for a cause. To have that respect and adoration transformed into contempt and dishonor may cause you to crumble inside, feeling as if there is nothing to hold you up or to keep you going. In fact, this is what the phrase "falling from grace" often implies. In addition to the connotation of falling from the grace of God, the phrase refers to being *disgraced,* or to being found *unacceptable* to those we need to accept us the most. In other words, to be disgraced is to be despised and rejected by our own. This is the shame we all fear the most.

As Lewis Smedes states:

> Shame digs deeper when it is our own people who reject us, who shame us because they feel shamed by us. . . . When we were children, if one of us did something nasty, we would set him aside, point our fingers at him, and sing this ditty:
> *Shame, shame, double shame.*
> *Everybody knows your name.*[6]

This goes back to the primitive belief that a person's name stands for what people believe he is. When a person "loses his good name" it means his name is one of shame.

Richard Berendzen

There are probably few occasions when the shame you feel is worse than having your name splashed across a

---

[6] Smedes, 56.

newspaper in derogatory headlines. This is the agony that
Richard Berendzen, past president of American University
in Washington D.C., had to endure as part of his fall from
grace. You may remember reading about his case in the
newspapers a few years ago. He wrote about his experience in his book, *Come Here.*

"It's on page one again. I hate to have to read this to
you."

"Go ahead."

"Are you sure you're ready?"

"Well, if the world knows, so should I."

" 'Obscene Phone Calls Are Traced To AU President.' "

"Oh, God!" Sweat poured off my head. My pulse
raced. My veins felt like they'd burst.

[His wife] Gail's voice was quiet but steady.

" 'Richard E. Berendzen abruptly resigned this month
as president of American University while Fairfax County
police are investigating obscene phone calls that led
directly—and unexpectedly—to the president's private
phone, informed sources said yesterday.' "

I gagged and threw up on the floor. I couldn't speak,
so, after a pause, Gail kept on reading.

" 'The investigation began several weeks ago, when
Fairfax police received several complaints, some of them
from people employed in daycare or babysitting-related
jobs, about dirty calls, according to an informed source.

" 'The source said that the caller in question, in telephone conversations with the adult women daycare
providers, made inappropriate or sexually oriented comments about children under their care.

" 'Berendzen has not been charged with any crime.' "

"Gail, wait a minute. I've got two daughters, a wife,
students, the university, and on page one of the

Washington Post it says I've made sexually oriented comments about children? Oh, God! My God . . ."[7]

Social shame can be a shield against our worst
impulses. Those who feel no shame are indeed in trouble
because they are deceiving themselves into believing that
they have nothing to be ashamed of. What keeps us from
our darker impulses is often less the fear of God's judgment and more the fear of the judgment of our peers.

But taking on the shame projected on us by others and
allowing that shame to define us is also dangerous. As Al
Pacino is quoted as saying, "I am somewhat better and
somewhat worse than my reputation."

Being shunned or rejected by others causes more than
shame; it causes debilitating shame. Jane Middelton-Moz
defines debilitating shame as:

> an isolating experience that makes us think we are
> completely alone and unique in our unlovability. It is a
> feeling that we are intensely and profoundly unlovable.
> Debilitating shame is a state of self-hate and self-
> devaluation that is comparable to little else.
>
> When we experience debilitating shame, all reality
> perspective is lost and we feel that all of our vulnerabil-
> ities become exposed and magnified. We believe that
> others in our world view us with disdain and/or disgust.[8]

While others may criticize, judge or even shun you, the
important thing to remember is that what *you* think about

---

[7] Richard Berendzen, *Come Here* (New York: Villard Books, 1993), 149.
[8] Middelton-Moz, 16-17.

yourself is far more important than what others think. If you are willing to perceive your fall as an opportunity to learn from past mistakes and work toward becoming a better person, if you are willing to handle your fall with honesty and integrity, then in the long run you will see that it doesn't really matter what others think, say or do regarding your fall. What matters is what *you* think, say and do, and what kind of person you end up becoming in the process.

Dealing with Your Anger

It is natural for you to feel angry about your fall. After all, you are probably dealing with a great deal of loss. Loss of income, status, adoration, perhaps even the loss of your livelihood, your career or your marriage. You may feel angry at the people you hold responsible for your fall (the person who filed suit against you, the woman who exposed the affair you were having, your spouse for wanting so many material possessions). You may even feel angry with God for forsaking you. But eventually, you are going to have to face the truth. You and only you are responsible for your fall. As painful as this will be to face, it is the only way you are going to survive your fall and receive its many blessings.

You will probably fight this truth for a long time by insisting that it is really someone else's fault or by continuing to live in a fantasy world of "if only's." "If only I didn't get caught." "If only she had kept her big mouth shut." But if you're lucky, eventually the truth will slowly begin to seep into your consciousness, as it did with Megan.

Megan

Megan is in prison serving a three-and-a-half-year sentence for mail fraud and conspiracy. How did she get there? On the surface it would appear that she was an innocent victim, that her arrest and subsequent incarceration were due to a misunderstanding, a miscarriage of justice. Megan's explanation follows:

"I was originally hired as a secretary for a financial company. They acted as a middleman for people with poor credit who were seeking a loan or debt consolidation. I did so well that I was offered the job of office manager with a substantial pay increase within the first year. Unbeknownst to me, I was working for a fraudulent company, and one day the postal inspector arrived at our office and shut us down. Even though I didn't have any idea that the company I was working for was running a telemarketing scam, I was indicted for mail fraud and conspiracy.

"I'll never forget the day they came to arrest me. I was dumbfounded. I'd been cooperating with the government all along, answering all their questions, providing them with all my records. I had no idea they'd actually arrest me.

"My entire family has been humiliated by this. It's been in all the papers, of course, and in the local news. Those who don't really know me probably think I'm guilty. I think some of my friends even wonder. I have a 10-year-old daughter who is afraid to go to school every day because she's been teased and taunted by the kids so much. And the worst part about it is that I have another child, a four-year-old son, who is going to be without his mother for the next three and a half years—that is, unless I get out on appeal.

"At first I was just bitter and angry, blaming everyone but myself. Of course, I was angry with my boss and the other crooks who got me into this mess. But I was also enraged with the investigators and the government for not recognizing that I was a victim too, and for not believing me when I told them I didn't know we were scamming people.

"But eventually, I had to start realizing that there had been signs, indications that maybe things weren't on the up-and-up. But I didn't want to see them. I didn't want to admit it to myself because I was making such good money.

"The truth is, it was greed that got me into this mess. Wanting to have a new car and great clothes for me and my kids. Wanting to impress people. Well, I sure impressed them when I got arrested, all right.

"When I finally faced it all, I got really depressed. I couldn't help thinking about what I'd done to my kids—Tammy being so humiliated at school and Jason without a mother, when he is such a little thing. And my husband; I couldn't believe what I'd done to my husband. Left all alone raising two kids . . . being ashamed because he has a criminal for a wife."

Taking responsibility may require an attitude adjustment on your part. You may have a tendency to blame others for your problems or consider yourself a victim of circumstances. But this has to stop. Starting right now, you need to begin to accept responsibility for your actions, no matter what the circumstances. That is the only way you are going to reap any blessings from your fall, the only way you are going to come out of this unfortunate situation a better person.

Some of you may have been victimized earlier in your life in some way and therefore perceive yourself as a victim today. But having been a victim in the past does not mean that you have to remain a victim in adulthood. And having been a victim does not mean that you are completely pure, innocent and incapable of being a victimizer yourself. You may have learned to stand up for yourself at the expense of others, or you may have reenacted your abuse by victimizing others. You may have become so pompous and judgmental of others that you forget that you, too, can make mistakes, are sometimes inconsiderate, selfish, and yes, even abusive.

Facing the truth about your situation and taking responsibility for your part in it is not the same as *blaming* yourself. Taking responsibility will empower you, make you feel less hopeless, less like a victim. It will be the first step in the healing process. Blaming yourself, on the other hand, will only cause you to dig yourself into a deeper hole and will actually prevent you from healing.

Dealing with Depression

Once you have faced the truth about who is responsible for your fall, you may experience depression, as Megan did. Most, if not all, of those who have a fall experience a depression, sometimes mild, sometimes severe. If you think about it, how can you fall off a pedestal or fall from the heights of ecstasy, wealth or fame without reacting to the fall? For some the drop isn't so far, for others it is a long way down. Usually, the farther you fall, the deeper the depression.

We have all encountered the symptoms of depression: sadness, dejection, gloom, boredom or feeling the "blahs." Different people describe feeling depressed in different ways, but in normal states of depression we can usually discover the causes and cope with the depression with tactics we have learned to use in the past. Sometimes we do things to take our mind off it, such as taking a walk, reading a book or watching television. Other times we recognize that we need to gain a new perspective, so we talk it out with a friend or just wait it out, knowing that it will pass.

But the type of depression you are likely to experience as a result of a fall from grace cannot be handled in any of the above ways, at least not successfully. There are three types of depression you are likely to feel due to your fall.

1. Depression caused by the repression or suppression of emotions

When you deny emotions such as anger or pain, you turn off other feelings as well. We can't just pick and choose which emotions we are going to allow ourselves to feel without affecting our ability to feel and express *all* our emotions: the so-called positive ones—joy and love—as well as the so-called negative ones—anger, pain, fear, guilt and shame.

2. Clinical depression

A major depressive episode is characterized by:

   a. Dysphoric mood—characterized by symptoms such as feeling depressed, sad, blue, hopeless, low, down in the dumps, irritable.

   b. Apathy—loss of interest or pleasure in all or almost all usual activities and pastimes.

   c. At least four of the following symptoms present nearly every day for a period of at least two weeks:

- Poor appetite or significant weight loss (when not dieting), or increased appetite or significant weight gain
- Insomnia or hypersomnia
- Psychomotor agitation or retardation (not merely subjective feelings of restlessness or being slowed down)
- Loss of interest or pleasure in usual activities, or decrease in sexual drive
- Loss of energy, fatigue
- Feelings of worthlessness, self-reproach, or excessive or inappropriate guilt
- Complaints or evidence of diminished ability to think or concentrate, such as slowed thinking, or indecisiveness
- Recurrent thoughts of death, suicidal ideation, wishes to be dead, or suicide attempt

This is how Richard Berendzen described his experience of clinical depression:

The next few days became a blur, as I slid into clinical depression. No horror, no hell can equal it. Beyond any physical pain I'd ever known, this agony permeated all of me. I wanted only to stay in my room with the lights off, drapes drawn, and door shut. I wanted to close in on myself, just as a dying star becomes a black hole.

. . . Depressed and scared by my utter absence of a will to live. My insides felt rotted. . . . I cared about

no one and no one cared about me. . . . My misery
was exacerbated by the inescapable fact that I had
brought this on myself. It was all my fault.

The metaphor that kept coming back was a free-fall.
I could see myself falling, falling, falling to the center
of the Earth. I thought I had found hell. But would the
fall ever end? I kept waiting to hit bottom. How far
down could I fall? Each time I thought I was there, I
found another level lower. If I could just hit bottom, I
might be able to begin the long climb out of the hole. [9]

3. Abandonment depression

In his book, *The Search for the Real Self:
Unmasking the Personality Disorders of Our Age,*
James F. Masterson, M.D., explains that abandonment depression is actually an umbrella term that
includes depression, panic, rage, guilt, helplessness
(hopelessness) and emptiness (void). The intensity
of these six feelings can become unbearable, creating a panicky state of helplessness, of feeling out
of control, and a relentless need to feel protected
and safe again.

According to Masterson, abandonment depression
is far more devastating than the forms of depression
that come and go in the course of our daily lives. In
the throes of abandonment depression, a person will
feel that part of his very self is lost or cut off from
the supplies necessary to sustain life. Many people
experience it as similar to losing an arm or a leg.

---

[9] Berendzen, 156, 160, 162.

Others experience it as feeling deprived of oxygen. As they teeter on the brink of despair, many feel like giving up. Thoughts of suicide are quite common.

As Masterson explains, abandonment depression and rage go hand-in-hand. As your depression intensifies and comes to the surface, so will your anger. Aside from your anger at your situation, your rage may be rather diffuse and you may feel angry at life and everyone in it. Although this anger is normal, you will need to find ways to control your angry responses in those situations where it would not be appropriate to indulge it.

According to Masterson:

Anger that is part of the abandonment depression, however, has more damaging consequences. This anger is long-lasting, building up from painful childhood experiences that may not be easily recalled because they are too solidly defended against.

The more depressed you become, the more angry you may get. Eventually the real source of your anger is uncovered such as from early in your childhood when your real self was trying to emerge and failed to do so. When the rage reaches a peak, a person can actually entertain homicidal fantasies. As suicide seemed appropriate for the bottoming out of depression, so homicide seems to be the only solution when anger and rage reach the levels beyond which they can no longer be endured. [10]

---

[10] James F. Masterson, M.D., *The Search for the Real Self: Unmasking the Personality Disorders of Our Age* (New York: The Free Press, 1988), 64, 65.

Now That We Have Your Attention

As painful and debilitating as depression can be, it is actually one of the first steps to healing and one of the blessings of a fall.

If you are like many people who experience a fall, you have probably built a fairly strong defense system to protect yourself from pain, doubt and fear. Perhaps you learned early in your life that you couldn't depend on others, that you were essentially alone in the world. You may have had to "toughen up" after years of neglectful or abusive treatment by your parents, other caretakers or lovers. You may have determined early on that in order to reach your goals you needed to block out all other distractions, including your emotions.

Those of us who experience a fall are a unique group of people. While it may seem like anyone can experience a fall, if you think about it, in order to fall you must reach a certain height. The higher you reach, the farther you have to fall. Those who do not aspire to great heights may experience a *setback* from time to time, but they probably don't experience a full-fledged fall.

In order to reach the heights of fame, wealth, celebrity, adoration or recognition, you probably had to work hard to get there. You had to keep your eye on the prize and not get distracted by other things (relationships, petty problems, your emotions and those of others). That kind of focus creates a certain personality: someone who doesn't give up easily, but also someone who doesn't reach out for help easily; someone who is tough, but perhaps a little too tough when it comes to his own feelings and the feelings of others.

Experiencing a fall from grace can put a chink in your armor and cause you to feel more vulnerable than you are used to feeling. This crack in your facade can be the first glimpse you have had of your soul, your essence. It may be the pathway to discovering who you really are. Ironically, your newly experienced vulnerability—the feeling that you are now exposed for all the world to see, that all your weaknesses are now visible—is the very thing that can save you. It is the very thing that will allow you to admit you need help.

The Alcoholics Anonymous phrase, "You have to reach bottom before you can start to get better," was written with you in mind. You've hit bottom—big time. And this is truly a blessing in disguise. If you are like I am, you need to be hit over the head before you pay attention. Some people are able to heed the warnings. Not me. The roof has to fall down around me before I realize it's time to do something.

This is your wake-up call. Take it and be grateful you got it. Otherwise, no telling where you would have ended up.

Reaching Out for Help

If you are experiencing any form of severe depression, it is important that you seek help. You cannot just will yourself out of a depression. By its very nature, depression takes away your will and your motivation, and distorts your perception. You may need medication, at least temporarily, especially if you feel suicidal. More important, you need someone to talk to, someone who is not involved personally in your life, someone who can provide an objective perspective.

If you feel you are suffering from the first type of depression, the one caused by holding in your feelings, you will need to give yourself permission to feel and express all your emotions without censoring yourself. For example, even though you now know you are responsible for your fall, it's still okay to be angry about it, to feel the pain of it, and to even feel sorry for yourself at times.

The most common defense against feelings is intellectualization. When we intellectualize we seek reasons to explain, analyze, censor and judge our feelings. We tell ourselves that certain feelings are bad or wrong and therefore we shouldn't feel them. Or we tell ourselves that feelings are childish and that those who express them openly are foolish. But while our emotions can sometimes be unpleasant, confusing, untimely and even disruptive, they are as natural as any other body function and as necessary. You may need help to work past your tendency to intellectualize your emotions, and help to begin allowing yourself to express your emotions in constructive ways.

Most people do not seek therapy until there is a crisis, and I am sure you are no exception. You are probably a very strong-willed, independent person who is not used to reaching out to anyone. Hopefully, your fall has softened you a bit and made you realize you can't do it alone. Sometimes, that is the biggest blessing of all.

Now that you are humbled, now that your armor has a slight chink in it, you can begin to look at what brought you to this place. There couldn't be a better time for you to seek help because you aren't feeling as defended or defensive as you normally are. You'll be more open to suggestion. You won't have to waste a lot of time trying to impress those who are trying to help you. That's over. You've hit bottom and now if you're smart you'll take the hand that is reaching out to help pull you up.

I can't tell you what kind of help you need. I certainly recommend individual psychotherapy. But you may also need to join a support group or a 12-Step program. If your fall is alcohol-related, you know where you need to go. But you may not know that there are 12-Step programs for other problems as well. For example, if your fall was related to sexual acting out or compulsive sexual behavior, check out Sex Addicts Anonymous. If your fall was created by abusing your body through overeating, check out Overeaters Anonymous. There is also Gamblers Anonymous and Debtors Anonymous. I provide a complete listing of resources at the end of this book.

If you don't feel you're ready to seek outside help, continue reading the book. It will certainly help you to feel less alone to learn about the experiences of others. And reading about the blessings others experienced from their fall will give you hope, something you desperately need at this time. It will help you to continue looking inside yourself for your own answers and to look to your creator for guidance. Hopefully, part of that guidance will be to put your pride aside and reach out for help. It's up to you.

3 Helping Your Loved Ones to Cope

It's odd that you can get so
anesthetized by your own pain or your
own problem that you don't quite fully share the hell
of someone close to you.

LADY BIRD JOHNSON

It's important to get out of your skin
and into somebody else's.

DIANE ARBUS

I n spite of the many blessings that can come from a
fall, there are negative consequences that need to be
dealt with. The most significant consequence is recognizing how your fall from grace has affected those who
care about you and who, in essence, must go through
your fall with you.

One of the first things you will need to handle is how
you are going to deal with your family. You'll undoubt-
edly want to protect them from experiencing the humiliation and shame of your fall. You may even try to hide
the entire situation from them. This is understandable.
You love them and don't want them to suffer.

But one of the blessings from your fall can be an
improved relationship with your family. How can your
relationship with your family be *improved* by your fall?
Because it will give you a chance to:

- Get closer to your family
- Come clean about who you really are
- Give your family the chance to support you
- Mend some fences
- Work with your family to resolve the problem

Dealing with a Scandal

The best way of coping with the shame that shadows
you is to deal with it head-on. Since your family will
eventually hear about your fall one way or another, do
you really want to live each day in fear of them finding
out? And since they are most likely going to find out
anyway, wouldn't you rather they hear it from you than
from someone else?

Hiding the truth from family and friends is not the way to protect them. It only makes them more vulnerable to pain once they hear the truth from someone else. And if you're honest with yourself, you're probably not keeping the truth from them to protect them as much as to avoid having to deal with their reactions once they find out.

It is, of course, understandable that you want to protect your family from scandal and disappointment. Ironically, the best way to do this may be to make certain they hear the truth from you instead of hearing rumors or exaggerations from another source. One advantage to telling your family yourself is that you will be able to choose the time and place for your revelation.

Another advantage is that it will probably hurt less for them to hear it from you, and you will be right there to comfort them and answer their questions. Your family will respect you a great deal more for having the courage to face them with the truth.

This is how Richard Berendzen told his wife about his fall from grace:

> I stepped into a private office, paused for a moment, and then called my wife—that loving, rational, and trusting person. She answered at once. "Bunny," I began with my usual pet name for her, "if I ever needed you, I need you now. I'm here with four trustees and Tony. I've made some phone calls, which the police are investigating. And I've resigned the presidency."
>
> "What?" she gasped. "Are you okay?"
>
> I told her I was and that somehow we'd come through this. We'd have to be strong. Then, with a breaking voice,

I whispered, "I love you, Bunny. And I'm so very sorry. Forgive me."[1]

But Richard didn't tell his wife the details of his calls. Nor did he tell her that he had been sexually abused by his mother.

While in treatment at the Sexual Disorders Clinic of the world-renowned Johns Hopkins Hospital, instead of being able to focus on his own treatment, he agonized over people finding out.

> What if my daughters found out, or our friends? My humil-
> iation and shame weighed me down like cement. I could
> bear the feelings only because I felt confident that the real
> story of my resignation would remain private.[2]

And he didn't tell his daughters about his fall. It wasn't until he knew the story was due to come out in the *Washington Post* that he had his wife, Gail, fly to Boston where their daughter Natasha was attending school. They were worried that reporters would get to Natasha before Gail did, and for good reason. Someone who had an early edition of the *Post* called Natasha at midnight at her dorm and asked her about her father's "alleged improprieties." Natasha didn't know what that meant, so the man gave her examples—things like stealing the university's money and drug abuse. She was shocked and hung up. A woman also called to try to get Natasha to tell her all she knew. Vultures were preying on their daughter.

---

[1] Richard Berendzen, 89.
[2] Ibid., 106.

When Gail told their other daughter, Debbie, her immediate response was, "Is that it? I had visions of him having tubes up his nose and being hooked up to machines. I've been terrified." She'd imagined scenarios far worse than what had actually happened.

When you do tell family members, it will be important to put your feelings aside long enough to think of their needs. Although telling your family will be extremely painful and will no doubt cause you to feel all sorts of pent-up emotions, you need to be aware of the effect the news will have on family members. You may even want to spend some time anticipating how each family member will react.

This is especially important when telling younger children the news. For example, you may know that your oldest son will more than likely react with anger to your news that you are going to have to file bankruptcy and return the new car, while your daughter is likely to be understanding and want to help in any way she can. Anticipating how your children will react can help prepare you for their reactions and prevent you from overreacting. For example, if you know ahead of time that your son may become angry, you won't be as likely to be hurt by his reaction or retaliate in anger yourself. Instead, you can take a deep breath and try to be understanding of his position.

Although you will no doubt feel relieved by your revelation and touched by any comfort and understanding, it would be incredibly selfish of you to expect your children to comfort you in your pain instead of you providing the comfort *they* need. If your daughter comes over to you and hugs you and says, "Don't worry, Daddy, we'll be all right," that is wonderful. But don't forget that underneath her desire to help you is a child who is having her own reactions, a child who needs comforting herself. Tell her, "Thank you, honey," and then ask her how *she* is feeling about what you've told her.

Most important, look to adults for comfort and support, not children. There is a fine line between letting your children know what is going on and allowing them to take the adult role of comforting you, but you will need to draw that line and not cross over it.

Richard Berendzen, who had been reluctant to talk to his children about his troubles, did come through for them in the end. When he called his daughter Natasha at school, he was focused on consoling her, not on being consoled by her.

> "Are you all right?"
>
> "Yes. . . . My friends are calling and coming to my room to say they support me."
>
> "I'm glad of that," I tried to console her. "I'm truly sorry for all this, Natasha. Please know that I love you dearly. This may get rugged for a while. But we'll pull through it. The doctors are taking good care of me. I'll be okay. So don't worry. Do you think you'll be all right?"[3]

Telling the Truth

It is vital that you tell the absolute truth when relating to your family and friends the reasons for your fall. If

---

[3] Berendzen, 148.

they are going to be able to stand by you and help you, they need to know the entire story. And they need to know what they are facing. Family and friends will probably respect you for coming clean, no matter what you've done. Now is not the time to try to save face or to tell only half-truths.

If you lie or tell a watered-down version of the story, you set yourself up for an even greater fall once the truth comes out. If you tell a version of the story that is more favorable to you, and your family and friends find out the truth, they will probably never trust you again. Your fall may have already tested the limits of their trust. Why risk severing a relationship over a lie?

This is not the time for excuses of any kind. Don't blame someone else for your problems, don't blame the economy or the stress you've been under, or the fact that you were trying to make money for your family. Don't try to make your family feel guilty because they spent the money you made, or make your family and friends feel guilty because they didn't notice how much stress you were under.

Admitting what you did, first to your family and friends, and later to your accusers, will do more than anything else to take the energy out of the situation.

PART II

WHY PEOPLE FALL FROM GRACE

Understanding
Why People Fall

People who fight with fire usually
end up with ashes.

ABIGAIL VAN BUREN

Whatever you may be sure of,
be sure of this: that you are dreadfully
like other people.

JAMES RUSSELL LOWELL

Whether your fall was caused by impulsiveness, a misuse of power, poor judgment or circumstances beyond your control, you can learn how to make something positive out of it and the rest of your life. To do this you must discover what caused your fall and the role you played in creating it. You and those close to you need to understand why it occurred.

For every Bob Packwood, Mike Tyson or Michael Jackson, there are hundreds of other less visible people who have fallen from less prominent pedestals for less dramatic reasons. There are those who have experienced a financial fall caused by overspending, speculation, gambling or mismanagement. People who were once financially secure have lost homes, property, businesses, sometimes everything. Others have experienced a fall created by impulsiveness, addictions or grandiosity. Many who experience a fall are victims of the excesses of the 1980s—drug addiction, sexual promiscuity, financial speculation. Others are victims of their own personalities and character disorders.

Who Is Most Likely to Fall?

While anyone can have the experience of falling from grace, certain types of people tend to be more likely to fall:

1. The celebrity or ultra-successful person
2. The powerful
3. The "all good" person

4. The addict (alcohol, drugs, food, sex, gambling, shopping, etc.)
5. Those with narcissistic tendencies
6. Those who have unfinished business from the past

More than likely, you fall into at least one if not more of the above categories. Often these categories overlap. Certainly there is overlap in terms of successful people also being powerful. In the following section I'll elaborate on each category, including why these people are most likely to fall.

1. The Ultra-successful Person or the Celebrity

There are several reasons why famous people and the ultra-successful are prone to a fall. First of all, with fame comes enormous pressure, a loss of privacy and the envy of others. It takes a tremendously strong individual to be able to cope with these three hazards.

It is also difficult, if not impossible, for the famous to live up to the persona thrust upon them by others. They are expected to be superhuman and not to suffer from human frailties such as insecurity, laziness, gluttony or infidelity. Although the famous are no different from other people, they are treated as if they are a breed apart and are judged especially harshly.

Of these hazards, envy is perhaps the most dangerous. Fame and wealth often create a tremendous amount of envy in others. If jealousy is the green-eyed monster, then envy is the dreaded vampire sucking the blood, the very life force from its victims, destroying

them in the process. Those who envy others' possessions, good qualities, lifestyle and loved ones ultimately
want to destroy their victims and take over their lives.
They envy the talents of others because they have no
idea how much work it takes to become an expert, a
virtuoso, a success. They feel that success was just
given to the other person.

Envy can cause people to make up malicious gossip
and to try to sabotage the success and happiness of
those they envy. Group envy can be especially crushing.
Those who are famous and envied by a large number of
people can become overwhelmed by its poisonous
power. There are several ways the famous try to cope
with envy directed toward them.

1. *Counter-attack:* They become as destructive and
   hateful as those who envy them.
2. *Internalize the blame:* They take on the blame and
   begin to believe what is said about them. This especially happens when a group makes a scapegoat of
   an individual.
3. *Deny the parts of their personality that others envied:*
   Because they lack the courage to embrace those
   parts of themselves that others envy, the famous
   often devalue or disown their gifts or talents.

If fame comes suddenly, or to the young or inexperi-
enced, it is often more than the average person can
handle. This is why we hear so often about the falls of
those considered to be "overnight successes." If you
were a fairly balanced, grounded person to begin with,

success and adoration might not go to your head; but if you were insecure and suffered from low self-esteem before your rise to fame, the adoration of others and your newly found wealth and success can cause you to overcompensate for your basic insecurity by becoming conceited and arrogant.

Another reason why the famous often fall is because of unhealthy shame. When you are shame-bound, the recognition, adoration and money that come from fame and celebrity can feel extremely uncomfortable. Those who are shame-bound continually feel as if they are a fake and a phony, and that if the people who admired them really knew who they were, these same people would feel nothing but contempt for them.

This is what happened with Michele Pillar Carlton, a three-time Grammy-nominated Christian recording artist.

Michele Pillar Carlton

Michele came from an extremely abusive, neglectful home where her parents *and* her siblings were abusing drugs and alcohol. She was overwhelmed with shame.

"My mother's mood swung from complete unaware-ness as to what I might be doing, to beating me stringently for leaving my shoes in the living room. I was too young at the time to understand that the mayhem at home was the product of parents and siblings who were abusing drugs and alcohol.

"All I knew was that we didn't have top sheets. We didn't even have bottom sheets most of the time. A blanket thrown over the bed would have to do. Of course, I was surely to blame for the unmade bed because I was still wetting the bed from time to time and sucking my thumb at the ripe old age of nine.

"My thumb had pushed my front teeth out so far that one boy at school told me that I could eat corn through a picket fence. My bangs were always cut crooked and my school dresses worn wrinkled unless I ironed that morning."

This shame-filled child grew up to become a famous Christian singer who appeared on stage with great evangelists such as Billy Graham and Dr. Robert Schuller.

"The more I appeared with people of such incredible strength, the more I feared my true identity might be revealed. I'd read articles about myself in magazines and felt as though I needed to emotionally catch up with my own publicity.

"I was physically, emotionally and spiritually getting very tired. The ironic part of this is that I wasn't doing anything wrong, but I felt like my past was chasing me and that my off-kilter beginning would one day catch up with me."

And indeed it did. Michele committed what she calls "professional suicide" by committing adultery with her producer. If she had been a pop singer, nothing much would have come of this aside from some tabloid gossip, but in the Christian music industry, it was disaster.

"Quietly and coldly, I was soon dropped from my record label and lost my personal manager. I was the talk of every church's office staff throughout America, but I was down from the high wire and that somehow felt more honest to me."

Michele now recognizes that it was a desperate move. She also realizes she had deliberately chosen behavior she knew would ruin her career.

"I ended up back at my mother's house—the birthplace of my shame. My career was ended. I felt like committing suicide.

"I needed to stop and take the time and understand my humble beginnings, to separate the truth from the lies of it all. I now know I could have accomplished this task without blowing up my whole life, but I didn't know how then."

My own fall was caused in part by the limited fame I experienced after my first book was published. On one hand, it fed my narcissistic tendencies to be on *Oprah!*, *Donahue* and *Sally Jesse Raphael,* as well as other television and radio programs. But on the other hand, the adoration scared me. I, too, had a tremendous amount of unhealthy shame. Mine was caused by a shaming mother and childhood sexual abuse and I, too, kept waiting to be "found out."

2. The Powerful

You've probably heard the saying, "Power corrupts." In fact, throughout history we have witnessed this phenomenon so often that the saying has become a truism. Like fame, achieving a great deal of power, especially when it is power over others, causes a person to lose touch with reality. The powerful begin to believe that they are special, that they are not required to treat those under them with the respect they would show their so-called equals.

Ironically, those who abuse their power the most are often those who did not experience much personal power when they were younger. The more power they acquire, the better they seem to feel about themselves. In reality, though, the good feelings are short-lived and the craving for more power returns.

Power is very seductive. The more power we obtain, the more we want. Soon our entire existence is dictated by the hunger for more power. Nothing else seems to matter as much—not our relationships, not how others feel. Under these conditions, it is no wonder that the powerful often fall.

3. The "All-Good" Person

Those who try to be consistently good, kind, understanding and magnanimous are in grave danger of falling. Trying to be good *all* the time is like walking a tightrope. No one can stay up there forever. One false move and you come crashing down. We are all made up of a combination of both good and bad qualities. When we deny our so-called bad qualities, they usually end up emerging from us when we least expect them.

4. The Addict

Those who are addicted to alcohol, drugs, sex, food, gambling, shopping or something else are prime candidates for a fall. It is just a matter of time before an addiction takes over your life, causing you to lose your job or business, your marriage or relationship, or causing you to break the law or get involved in a scandal.

5. Those with Narcissistic Tendencies

Narcissism has not received as much attention as other disorders in our society, and yet it is the cause of many falls and the core problem of many people who suffer from addictions. It has been called "the most hidden disorder of our time."

Most people misunderstand narcissism to be a condition that affects individuals who have high self-esteem and who think too highly of themselves. But ironically, it is those whose self-esteem is low who are the ones most likely to be narcissistic.

Narcissism is characterized by:

- A grandiose sense of self-importance
- Recurrent fantasies of unlimited success, power, brilliance, beauty or ideal love
- A craving for constant attention and admiration
- Feelings of rage, humiliation or haughty indifference when criticized or defeated

It is also characterized by at least two of the following:

- A sense of entitlement
- A tendency to exploit and take advantage of others, and to disregard their rights
- Oscillation between extreme over-idealization and devaluation of others
- Lack of empathy—not just an inability to recognize how others feel, but often an inability to realize that others have feelings at all

According to Dr. James Masterson, a leading expert on narcissism:

> On the surface the narcissist is brash, exhibitionistic, self-assured, single-minded, often exuding an aura of success in career and relationships. Narcissists often seem to be the people who have everything—talent, wealth, beauty, health and power, and a strong sense of knowing what they want and how to get it. [1]

The term *narcissist* comes from the Greek myth of Narcissus—a young man who fell in love with his own reflection mirrored in a lake. Unable to pull himself away from the contemplation of his own beauty, he eventually starved to death and fell into the water, never more to be seen. The person with a narcissistic personality disorder reenacts in his own life two key themes of the myth: he becomes totally absorbed in his own perfection and in striving for the narcissistic supplies that he needs to keep his image full-blown and intact. Beneath the grandiose false self is an impaired real self whose development has been arrested in an effort to protect against an abandonment depression (refer to the previous discussion on depression in chapter 2). The grandiose self guides the narcissist's feelings and behavior, obscuring or hiding the underlying impaired real self with its abandonment depression.

As he basks in the comfortable environment that he has created, life can seem pretty good to the narcissistic

---

[1] Masterson, 90.

person. As long as nothing infiltrates his cocoon, he will not be aware of any serious personality problems. He thinks he has it all, and those who know him will agree, since he has carefully selected them to be part of his world and thereby bolster his view of himself.

6. Those with Unfinished Business from the Past

Those who have not dealt with their past will probably discover that it *will* catch up with them. Often this occurs as a fall from grace. Unfinished business has a way of sneaking up on us, invading our lives in insidious ways, and chipping away at our confidence, our relationships and our success.

Imbalance—The Real Cause of a Fall

My premise is that a fall from grace does not and cannot occur unless there is tremendous *imbalance* in a person's life. This imbalance must be corrected in order for the person to heal and rise from his fall.

Exactly how can an imbalance in one area of your life create a fall? Let's start by defining the word *balance*. Used in this context, it means "mental and emotional steadiness." We invite a fall if we put too much emphasis on one area of our lives to the detriment of others. Whenever anything is off-balance it is precarious. Equilibrium and stability are created by symmetry and balance.

I have defined six types of imbalances. They include:

1. An imbalance of the heart
2. An imbalance of character
3. An imbalance of the body
4. An imbalance of power
5. An imbalance of "goodness"
6. An imbalance of the soul

Many people suffer from more than one type of imbalance. And in today's society, almost all of us suffer from an imbalance of the soul. But the likelihood is strong that just one imbalance was the major cause of your fall. One of the main goals of this book is to help you discover your particular imbalance and find the blessings that can come from this discovery.

In the next six chapters I will guide you step-by-step through this process. I will describe each type of imbalance and provide case examples that will further illustrate each. You will be able to see how a particular imbalance caused a fall and how the person came to recognize it as such. I am sure you will recognize yourself in at least one situation, perhaps more.

An Imbalance
of the Heart

Tears may be dried up, but
the heart—never.

MARGUERITE DE VALOIS

An imbalance of the heart is generally caused by one of the following:

1. Becoming cut off from your heart and your passion
2. Having your heart set on only one goal to the exclusion of everything else
3. Giving your heart away to someone who doesn't deserve it

In the first situation, people have lost touch with their emotions. They no longer know how they feel at any given time, and they may be in danger of losing their compassion and ability to empathize with others. In the extreme, they may appear almost robotic in their motions and in their interactions with others. They become more and more insensitive to the feelings and needs of others. Because they have hardened their hearts toward others, they may become more and more judgmental and critical. They may begin to have unreasonable expectations and make unreasonable demands of themselves and others. They may become difficult to please and seem to need more and more money, fame or success to compensate for their lack of connectedness to themselves and others.

Sometimes this hardening of the heart occurs because people have put other things like success and money ahead of their personal relationships. Ironically, at other times it is because they have seen so much pain and suffering that their hearts simply can't take any more. They shut down as a self-protective measure, shielding themself from further pain, as Andrea's story illustrates.

Andrea

Andrea had been a social worker in Chicago for nearly 15 years. Assigned to child protection services and responsible for investigating reports of child abuse and neglect, Andrea had seen more than her share of horror— infants beaten and sodomized, toddlers bruised and burned, children left alone in rat-infested squalor, the smell of urine reeking from the room. She had known children whose parents sold them into prostitution in order to get drugs, parents who had murdered their children in a fit of rage because they wouldn't stop crying, and fathers who regularly had sex with their daughters.

After witnessing atrocities such as these for so many years, Andrea could no longer empathize with their pain and agony. Instead, she shut down. After years of trying to change the system and trying to teach parents how to care for their children, she gave up.

"I finally realized that nothing was going to change," she said. "In fact, things just seemed to be getting worse. Drug use increased, and the drugs were becoming more powerful. Parents seemed to be getting more and more abusive, and it seemed like people were turning away from it all. I guess that's why I finally did, too.

"When I first started my job back in my late 20s, I was as idealistic as anyone. I was going to save these kids. I was going to make things better. But after years of hitting my head up against a brick wall, I realized I was just one person, just a drop in the bucket. I couldn't change anything. All I could do was recommend a child be taken away from her parents and then I couldn't guarantee she was going to be any better off.

"If you knew how many kids are abused in foster homes, how many kids are sexually used by personnel in orphanages and state-run facilities, you'd be shocked. Time after time I saw kids I'd pulled out of abusive homes end up being just as abused or worse in homes where they were placed in order to be safe.

"It got so I began to feel hopeless. I knew I was drinking too much, but I needed something to ease the pain. And it worked, too. As time went on I got more and more numb to it all. I guess that's why I turned my back on those kids. They're right, you know, that's what I did: I turned my back on them. Timothy wasn't the first, you know. There were others."

Andrea is referring to a case in which a three-year-old boy named Timothy was beaten to death by his mother; a mother who should never have had custody of him, a mother who had been reported several times to child protective services for abusing her son.

The people of Chicago were so shocked and outraged by Timothy's brutal death that an investigation was conducted to discover how such a thing could have happened. Andrea was publicly humiliated when a local news show identified her as the caseworker responsible for sending Timothy back to his abusive mother.

"This should have never happened and it wouldn't have happened if I'd been doing my job," she said. "It was an oversight on my part, a case of pure negligence.

"It was horrible when I heard what Timothy's mother had done to him. I couldn't believe it. I was in shock. I was so upset I couldn't go in to work for two days. I just sat in my apartment and stared out the window.

"When the investigation started, everyone at work assured me that I had nothing to worry about. 'Things like this happen,' they all said. 'It was nobody's fault. We're all just overworked. People slip through the cracks, that's all.'

"I wanted to believe them. I wanted to hide under all the excuses. We *were* overworked. We *did* have too many cases. No one could keep up with all the cases we had.

"My friends at work stood by me and said, 'Don't feel bad, it could have been any of us.' But when it came out on TV that I was the caseworker and reporters tried to interview me, I knew I was in trouble. People at work stopped talking to me. People in my neighborhood gave me dirty looks. Then my supervisor called me in and told me they were going to have to let me go. My whole world was crashing down on me. I didn't know what to do or where to turn. I felt horrible about the boy but I couldn't do anything to bring him back. And there was no one to talk to about it. It was the worst time in my life. I thought of suicide several times. I don't know how I got through it."

Rachel

Rachel suffered from the second type of imbalance of the heart—having your heart set on one goal to the exclusion of everything else.

Ever since she was a little girl, Rachel wanted to be an actress. She started acting in high school and was an active member in the National Thespians. At 18 she went to New York, got a job as a waitress to pay for acting classes, and joined a small theater group.

"I was determined to make it," said Rachel. "Nothing else mattered. I spent all my time and energy learning to be a better actor and going to auditions. My only friends were other actors and all we ever talked about was acting. I didn't have time for dating."

During the next few years, Rachel got some small parts in off-Broadway plays and garnered some good reviews. "It was just enough to keep me going. I didn't even make enough money as an actor to pay my rent, but I didn't care. When I didn't have a play, I'd work as a waitress and put money aside. I didn't even mind the rude customers or standing on my feet for eight-hour shifts as long as I could save enough money to bankroll me through another play."

But then money got tight, production slowed on off-Broadway plays, and Rachel didn't get a part for two years. "I got desperate and started thinking I'd better go to Hollywood," she said. "I hated to leave New York but times were bad. I figured I'd have a better chance in California, where they were still making lots of movies, so I packed up and got a ride out West.

"Things weren't any better out here [California]. If anything, competition for parts was even more fierce. And I wasn't a raving beauty like so many of the female actors are out here. I mean, I know I'm attractive, and I have an interesting face, but it seemed like they looked for knockouts out here more than in New York. In addition to working to pay the rent and going on one audition after another, I had to go to the gym every day to work out in order to keep up with the other actors."

To make matters worse, she had some unfortunate experiences with the "casting couch" and more than a few close calls with angry agents who tried to force themselves on her.

Four more years went by, with Rachel getting only a few small parts.

"I started getting really discouraged and tired of the constant struggle. I was 25 years old and I still hadn't gotten a major part. Even my agent started losing enthusiasm. And even when I was working, I wasn't happy. The part was too small. Or I was so tired from waitressing that I didn't do a very good job.

"It became clear to me that the business was less about talent than about surviving and sucking up to people. It was demeaning—trying out for parts I didn't even want, the constant rejection. I started realizing that I was missing out on life. I lived in a cheap apartment in Studio City, drove a clunker for a car and had no meaningful relationships, not even a close friend. I ate, breathed and slept acting, and it was getting old.

"As humiliating as it was, I decided to move back to my hometown. It was just awful at first, having to admit failure to everyone. I got my share of 'I told you so's' and put-downs by envious people. You know—'So, you're not better than us after all.' And it was very painful giving up my dream. It's what had been keeping me going for so many years. Now all I had was my job at my dad's office. I really hit a low point."

Lili

Lili is a good example of the third type of imbalance of the heart—giving your heart away to someone who doesn't deserve it. Lili had been alone for more than 10 years when she met Mark. In the beginning, she couldn't believe that a man this young and handsome could possibly find her attractive, but he soon convinced her that he found younger women boring. "How long do you think a pretty face can satisfy a man like me? I appreciate the kind of wisdom that a woman of experience has, the kind of culture that years of living well brings. You excite my mind as well as my body," he told her.

At first she was ashamed to introduce Mark to her friends. She knew they would be critical and suspicious of him, and she didn't blame them. After all, she knew he was probably attracted to her because of her money. But she also believed he really cared about her, and she enjoyed being generous with him.

After they'd been together for about six months, Lili felt

it was time to find out who her real friends were. She invited them all over for a party to meet Mark. She had grown to care for him so much that as far as she was concerned, those who accepted their relationship were friends, those who didn't were not.

The party went well. She overheard a few comments and saw a few raised eyebrows, but for the most part it seemed that the majority of her friends were as charmed by Mark as she was.

Soon, all invitations to dinners or parties included Mark. He became a welcome guest in the homes of all her friends, and they were often invited by other couples to the opera, ballet and major sporting events.

Mark was an entrepreneur and an inventor, and he often entertained Lili's friends by sharing with them his creative ideas. The men in particular enjoyed talking to him and shared in his enthusiasm for his latest invention—a high-tech juicer that was sure to revolutionize the fast-growing natural juice industry. He told them that one of the major commercial juicer chains was interested in his invention. They were all excited and happy for him. There was only one catch, he told them. He needed more money to refine his design. Money he just didn't have.

One by one, Lili's friends offered to invest in Mark's invention. They all made it clear that they didn't consider it a favor, but that they thought it appeared to be a sound business investment. They were going to be in on the ground floor of a booming business venture, and they had become almost as excited about it as Mark was.

Some invested only a few thousand dollars, others much more. Mark gave each investor a contract guaranteeing a certain percentage of the profits once the juicer was sold to the chain.

Lili had offered financial assistance many times to Mark, but he had always refused. Finally, he agreed to let her in on the deal since he only needed a few thousand dollars more.

At last, the design was modified and the juicer was ready. They had a wonderful celebratory dinner, just the two of them. Lili had never seen Mark so happy.

In fact, Lili never saw Mark again. He disappeared from her life overnight. She called his apartment, but there was no answer. She began to panic, thinking he'd been in an accident. But then she called his work number and discovered the phone had been disconnected. It didn't take her long to figure out what had happened. She'd been conned. Mark had used his connection with her to bilk all her friends out of thousands of dollars, money they would surely never see again.

She didn't know what to do. What was she going to tell her friends? She felt like such a fool. More than a fool: an accomplice. After all, she'd led him right to her friends.

Lili's first thought was to pay back all the money to her friends from her own savings. She'd make up some story that the deal had gone sour and that Mark was so depressed he couldn't see them himself. Then she'd say that he'd felt so defeated by his failure that he'd begun to drink, and she had to stop seeing him.

But she didn't know how much each person had invested, and it would probably leave her nearly penniless. And besides, she wanted him caught. She had to come clean.

She called the police, then called each one of her friends and told them the truth. It was the hardest thing she'd ever had to do in her life. She did it by phone because she couldn't bear to see their faces when she told them. Hearing their reactions on the phone was hard enough. First there was disbelief, then anger. Some became angry with her, others stayed focused on Mark and expressed pity for her. She didn't know which was worse, their anger or their pity.

"I've never been so humiliated in my life," said Lili. "I knew what they were all thinking: 'It's bad enough that she's a stupid old woman who's been conned by a man half her age, but did she have to expose us to him, too?'

"Word got around about what happened, and I got so I was ashamed to show my face socially. Some of my friends had stopped talking to me entirely and would ignore me if they saw me in public. Others spread malicious gossip about me that I would later hear from the few good friends who stuck by me. It was bad enough that I had to get over being used by Mark and feeling guilty about my friends' losses, but now I had to deal with complete strangers knowing my business. I felt like I just wanted to dig a hole and crawl into it.

"They even tried to vote me out of my country club when some of the people Mark had swindled complained and called for a vote. The last straw was when one of my friends went on a television show where they try to find criminals and told the whole sordid story, giving my name and everything. All my relatives and friends from school saw the show and called me. It seemed like the humiliation would never end."

As you can see from the examples, it is just as dangerous to allow your life to be dictated by your heart as it is to harden your heart. While we most certainly need to follow our heart and our passions, we must not do so to the exclusion of everything else in our lives. We need to strive for a balance between "following our heart" and being logical and rational; between sharing our heart with the one we love but not giving it away.

If you fit the description in the beginning of the chapter—or if you identified with either Andrea, Rachel or Lili—it is very likely that your fall was caused by an imbalance of the heart. As I stated earlier, though, your fall may have been created by several types of imbalances, so it is important that you continue reading the descriptions and examples of all the types of imbalances in the next several chapters.

An Imbalance
of Character

Some things are very important and some
are very unimportant. To know the difference is what
we are given life to find out.

ANNA F. TREVISAN

Always remember there are two types
of people in this world. Those who come into a room
and say, "Well, here I am!" and those who come in
and say, "Ah, there you are!"

FREDERICK L. COLLINS

Those individuals who have an imbalance in character have established inappropriate values, priorities and boundaries. They have begun to value money, power or prestige over such values as honesty, integrity and fairness. They consistently put their own needs before those of others. They often have a strong disrespect and disregard for the rights of others, even to the point where they may have broken the law. They may become controlled by their impulses and addictions. In order to feed their often insatiable needs for money, sex and power, they may have broken their own moral code and gone against their own values. Some have even established a moral code that does not resemble that of the average person.

There are certain psychological problems that predispose someone to having a character fall, the most significant being the character disorder known as narcissism, which I defined in a previous chapter.

The reason those with narcissistic tendencies are likely to fall is because there is never enough adoration, success or beauty to keep them happy, and they continually push the envelope or walk the edge in order to temporarily satisfy their insatiable needs. It is inevitable that they will crash and burn eventually, either because they stepped on one person too many to get what they wanted, or because their insatiable urges led them into some very dark waters.

In his book, *The Search For the Real Self,* Dr. James Masterson writes:

The narcissist is motivated by the continuous need for "supplies" to feed this grandiose conception of himself. "Supplies" here means quite specifically those activities and relationships that reinforce his grandiosity.

While most people value the admiration of others, that admiration is not their primary goal. Similarly, we all want to be in control, to succeed, and to do the best possible job. But healthy people value these objectives for their own sake and not merely as a means of obtaining admiration from others. To the outside observer, as well as to the narcissist himself who has not had treatment, these activities, such as spending an unusually great amount of time on one's work, appear to be realistically and appropriately motivated; that is, they seem to be engaged in for their own sake. However, this is an illusion. The motive is to use these activities to fuel the narcissist's need for perfection and uniqueness. [1]

Typically the narcissist is a restless person, pressured to keep moving in order to continuously reinforce his sense of grandeur. It's not uncommon for him to be a workaholic at a job he does well. Having nothing to do is threatening, since it does not meet his need for reinforcement or fit in with his self-image of being an achiever. This was the case with Max Sampson.

Max

For nearly two decades, Max Sampson was a powerful, confident, talented and highly successful movie director.

---

[1] Masterson, 91.

He started out as a stagehand but was able to work his way into the usually closed world of movie-making in only a few years, partly because of his creative, innovative ideas and partly because of his charisma and insatiable drive. With his enormous talent at self-promotion, he soon developed a reputation as someone who could produce a mega-hit, and before long he was rubbing elbows with some of Hollywood's most famous and infamous.

The same intensity that drove his work drove his play. He had a reputation as a womanizer, and became one of Hollywood's tolerated "bad boys."

"I wanted it all," he told me as he looked back on his life. "I loved being controversial. I wanted to be larger than life."

And he was. He became known almost as much for his conquests with women as he was as a director. He was linked with one scandal after another: jealous husbands coming home to find him in bed with their wives; rumored threesomes; bisexuality, and sadomasochism.

"Those were the early 1980s—you know, the days of cocaine and sex parties. Nearly everyone was doing it," he explained to me. But not everyone was doing it with as much flair and to such excess as he. "I was running away from some demons, all right. I didn't know what they were exactly, but I knew I was dealing with them the only way I could."

And then everything changed. With the end of the 1980s came the end of irresponsible sex, lavish spending and drug-induced sex parties. Max directed two failed movies, and the guys with the money began to doubt his talent. He'd stepped on lots of toes with his womanizing, and there were some embittered ex-husbands and jilted girlfriends who had it out for him. Suddenly he wasn't being hired to direct movies the way he had been.

"My entire identity was predicated on success. I panicked. I started calling up producer friends and asking them what they were working on, if they had anything for me. But time after time I was met with cold indifference. It was like I suddenly had the plague or something.

"I tried partying my troubles away, but things had changed. None of my friends were doing the drug/sex scene anymore. Hell, some of them were even going to Alcoholics Anonymous. They were all cleaning up their act and I didn't fit in anymore."

That's when Max crashed.

"I suddenly felt incredibly alone. I had no family, the guys I thought were my friends were giving me the cold shoulder and I wasn't working. I didn't know what to do with myself. I had no hobbies. Hell, I didn't even like sports. Work had been my life. Work and women. Sure, there were still women, but that was changing, too. Women weren't falling all over me like before. I wasn't a player anymore. I couldn't get them a job, I didn't have money to throw around. And the sex was just sex. There wasn't any real feeling.

"I suddenly realized I'd been running all my life to get somewhere and even after I got there, I'd kept on running. I think I was afraid to stop running because I was afraid I'd never start up again, and it was true. One day I just suddenly stopped trying. I stopped hustling for a project, I stopped going out. I just stayed in my bathrobe all day and watched TV or slept. I was so depressed, I stopped answering my phone.

"I'd wake up in the morning and look in the mirror and be overwhelmed with self-loathing. I chastised myself for being a lazy, good-for-nothing bum, but I just couldn't force myself to do anything.

"During those horrible months I came to realize that at the core of my life was a terrible emptiness that I'd been running away from all my life. I had nothing to do all day but be with the person I was most afraid to be with."

As is typical of someone suffering from this disorder, Max looked to others in his environment, and to his environment itself—clothes, cars, home, office—to reflect his exaggerated sense of importance. He surrounded himself with people who would appreciate and promote his best qualities and in this way proclaim to the world that he was unique, special and adored. When he no longer received enough supplies to justify this claim for himself, and when the mirroring from the environment became inadequate, his grandiose self became frustrated, and the underlying anger and depression emerged.

In reality, the narcissist's personality is based on a defensive false self that he must keep inflated like a balloon to avoid feeling underlying, hidden rage and depression. In fact, the narcissist's false self is characterized by an immunity to depression, and it is common for him to appear as if depression were simply not a part of his life.

As long as the false self is adequately buoyed up, it is the ballast that keeps him floating high, oblivious to frustration and depression.

The false defensive self is false in that it is based on a grandiose fantasy, rather than on reality. It is defensive in that its purpose is not to cope with or adapt to reality but to reinforce grandiosity in order to avoid feeling depressed.

Underneath this pursuit of mirroring and narcissistic feedback lies a massive denial of reality. He denies weakness in himself and the reality of depression altogether. Since he will not admit that his well-constructed environment can frustrate him, he cannot allow himself to be deflated by feelings of depression. He denies problems and setbacks, blaming them instead on the world in general or other people. He never considers that they might spring from a weakness in himself or a flaw in his self-concept. His conviction that he is special and omnipotent blinds him to any evidence that contradicts this conception of himself. For example, when a narcissist's wife leaves him, he does not get depressed; he gets angry. If he got depressed, he would be admitting weakness. Anger, on the other hand, implies that he has been wronged and hence is in the right; it can be viewed as a strength.

But should a severe crisis occur, one in which anger cannot displace depression, the narcissist may end up in therapy, where he will have to step out of his cocoon and try to activate his real self. It then becomes painfully apparent how impaired that self is in dealing with reality. When he tries to activate the real self to undertake an activity for its own sake (rather than for mirroring), or enter a relationship to care about the other person (rather than for mirroring), his facade crumbles and his real self-impairment is revealed. This was what had happened to Melody and what caused her to finally enter therapy.

Melody

From the time she was a little girl, Melody got attention for her good looks. She was a beautiful child with huge brown eyes, long thick eyelashes, curly auburn hair and a gorgeous smile. She charmed everyone, especially her father, who spoiled her shamelessly.

By the time Melody was a senior in high school, she was the envy of every girl and the heartthrob of every boy. She was a cheerleader, president of the drama club, and going steady with the best-looking boy in school.

After graduation from high school, Melody moved to New York, certain her looks would get her into a modeling agency. She was right. One of the major modeling agencies was so impressed with her, it took her on right away.

She was an overnight success. She modeled for major magazine ads, was a runway model for famous designers, and even appeared in a few television commercials. But it was all too much, too fast for Melody. She started drinking and taking drugs and soon had a reputation for being a bitch. She missed shoots and became so difficult that she lost some accounts. The designers were more tolerant of her bitchiness and treated her so much like a princess that she tried extra hard to please them.

But soon, even the designers had enough of her. Alcohol and drug abuse had made her so emaciated that even the best makeup could not enhance her appearance. At 21 she was already a has-been. Her agency refused to renew her contract, and others weren't interested in her.

She went to Europe to make a new start and for a while was fairly successful. She wasn't making as much money, but the photographers were happy to have a famous American model, and they treated her like royalty. But looking beautiful required money for clothes, hair stylists and health clubs. So soon she was dating rich men and allowing them to buy her things. She loved the adoration she got from the older men and didn't mind sleeping with them, especially when they bought her gorgeous clothes and jewelry.

There was a succession of men over the years—princes, movie moguls, millionaires—all of whom adored her and showered her with expensive gifts. Some were married, many were playboys, *all* were powerful. She traveled the world, lived in mansions, and rubbed elbows with the rich and famous. She drank too much, became addicted to cocaine, and often found herself in bed with more than one lover. Sometimes a threesome was made up of herself, her lover and another man; other times the third person was her lover's wife or girlfriend.

"I was flying high in the early 1980s, just like everyone else—too much partying, too much sex—but I was loving it," said Melody. "It suited my personality—more, more, more!"

But then something happened that Melody hadn't exactly planned on. "Sure, I'd put away plenty of money; after all, I wasn't stupid," she said. "But I had grown so used to getting everything I needed or wanted because I was beautiful that I was caught completely off guard when I reached 35. Suddenly, everything changed. Men didn't stop what they were doing when I walked by any longer. There was no longer a hush whenever I entered a room. And the rich and famous men who used to fall over themselves to get a date with me began to eye me coolly. And for the first time since high school, I didn't have a boyfriend.

"I panicked. I hired a personal trainer and started working out every day. I had collagen injected in my cheeks and upper lip to get rid of the lines that seemed to have appeared practically overnight. I became a strict vegetarian and started drinking tons of water.

"I took off about 10 pounds, and sculpted and toned my body to the point where it looked better than it ever had. I looked about 10 years younger. Men started looking at me again. Not that they ever really stopped, understand. It was more who was looking and how much they were impressed. I didn't go out with just anyone. He had to be either famous or rich, preferably both. And he had to be crazy about me.

"I got into another relationship, this time with a rich businessman. But the age thing had scared me. I'd never cared about marriage before, but now it became important. I wanted more emotional and financial security than just being some man's mistress for a few years. I became afraid of getting old and ending up all alone.

"About four months into the relationship I discovered the man I was madly in love with was married. I'd been with lots of married men in the past, but like I said, now it was different. He promised to leave his wife, but I knew better. I was heartbroken, but I left him. I wasn't going to waste my time waiting around for him.

"I don't know what happened after that, except that I started drinking too much and feeling sorry for myself. I'd really loved that guy and it wasn't so easy getting over him. I just wasn't bouncing back as well as I usually did.

"And then there was the whole thing with the movie. A past lover of mine, a director, called me up and told me he had a role for me in his next film. Joe said I was made for the part and he could almost guarantee me the job. I knew he still had a thing for me, but he assured me that his feelings for me had nothing to do with me getting the role.

"They were filming in Mexico and so we all went down there to begin shooting. It was hotter than hell and I hate the heat. I stayed in my trailer in front of a fan whenever I wasn't in a scene. I didn't have a big part, so I was in there a lot. There was another actor, Chad, a really young, handsome guy who also had a small part, and we'd sit in my trailer and drink iced tea and talk. Pretty soon we started up an affair, nothing serious, more a way of passing the time than anything else. I guess I was flattered that this gorgeous young hunk would find me attractive, but it didn't mean anything to me. I mean, he wasn't rich or anything.

"Well, anyway, to make a long story short, Joe got wind of the affair and blew his top. He started making fun of me in front of the crew, putting my acting down, telling me I was too old for the part. I was never so humiliated in my life. We got into a major screaming match in front of everyone. He said terrible things to me. 'You couldn't act your way out of a paper bag,' 'The only reason I gave you this job was because I felt sorry for you,' 'You're getting so old, I figured this was your last chance,' 'You're losing your looks fast, babe,' 'You can't even sleep your way to the top anymore.' I stormed off the set and got the first plane home.

"When I got home I fell into a deep depression. I kept hearing Joe's words, over and over in my head. I shut myself off from everyone, stopped going to lunch with friends or out on dates. I was afraid to go out to any of the restaurants I frequented for fear of being laughed at. I imagined everyone had heard about what had happened and that I was the laughing stock of the town. I just stayed in my apartment watching videos and sleeping, and getting more and more depressed.

"I stopped working out and gained so much weight I was ashamed to go out. It was a vicious circle. The longer I stayed in, the more depressed I got, and the more depressed I got, the more I ate. And I drank, too. One night I got so drunk I actually tried to shoot myself with a gun I keep in my apartment for protection. That's when I decided I'd better get help."

Not all narcissism is pathological. There is a distinction between healthy and pathological narcissism. Normal narcissism is vital for satisfaction and survival. According to Masterson, all the capacities of the real self come under the heading of normal narcissism, which in effect is the capacity to identify what you want and need, get yourself together and go after it, while also taking into account the welfare of others. That is the healthy way to feel good about yourself.

No one, not even Masterson, knows exactly what causes narcissism, but most experts agree that it, like most character or personality disorders, has its roots in early child-rearing practices. Like borderline personality disorder, narcissism is believed to be caused by faulty parental bonding, mirroring and caretaking.

What we do know for certain is that if a child receives healthy bonding, mirroring and caretaking in the first months and years of life, he or she will most likely *not* suffer from these debilitating disorders.

It is important to stress here that the individuals suffering from this disorder or these tendencies should not be blamed for the way they think and feel. It is not their fault. What they can be held responsible for is seeking professional help (and in some cases the assistance of 12-Step programs for related behavior such as alcoholism).

Once they become aware of how their behavior affects others, they can learn to modify and control it, "catch themselves in the act," so to speak, and become more caring human beings who are less controlled by their craving for beauty, success and acclaim, and more motivated toward connectedness and sharing with others.

An Imbalance of the Body

The body is the soul presented in its
richest and most expressive form.

THOMAS MOORE

An imbalance of the body is usually caused by one
of two things: either the neglect of the body and
its needs, or an overemphasis on the body to
the neglect of other aspects of one's life.

In the first situation, people are usually out of touch
with their bodily needs for rest, sleep, fresh air, exercise
and a proper diet. Or they may push their body to the
limit by overexercising, overeating or overworking.

They may engage in self-destructive behavior like smoking, starving their body, binging and purging, or alcohol or drug abuse. Addicts are notorious for having a fall due to the breakdown of their body caused by neglect and abuse. Because they have lost touch with their bodily needs and symptoms of distress, they are likely to experience a fall in the form of a physical illness or major accident. This was the case with Micky.

Micky

"For years I treated my body like it was a machine, expecting it to handle any abuse I gave it," said Micky. "I abused my body with alcohol, drugs, not enough rest, eating the wrong diet, you name it. I was young and I had a strong body and I thought I was invincible. But your body can take just so much abuse and then it starts to break down. And that's what happened to me.

"First, I started getting tired all the time. I thought I just needed to take it easy, try to eat right, and that did seem to help a little. But as soon as I felt better I went right back to my old ways. And sure enough, I started feeling bad again. I repeated the cycle of cutting back, feeling better, then starting up again several more times, until I finally went to the doctor. He ran a lot of tests and told me my liver was shot, my heart was damaged, and that if I didn't stop the drugs and drinking, I was going to kill myself.

"That really got to me. I told my wife what the doctor said and decided to quit cold turkey. Unfortunately, that only lasted a couple of weeks. You see, I'm a musician and I'm around drugs and alcohol all the time. So anyway, I went on this giant bender and didn't come home for a couple of days. When I finally made it home, my wife had packed up our two kids and was gone. She said in a note that she couldn't stand by and watch while I killed myself.

"At first I was furious with her. How dare she abandon me like that when I needed her the most? She hadn't even given me a chance. And how dare she take my kids, *my kids,* for Christ's sake. I loved those kids. I went on a real bummer and stayed drunk and drugged up for about a week. When I missed rehearsal, a couple of the guys from the band came over to see what was up and found me passed out, face down in my own vomit. When they couldn't revive me, even with CPR, they called an ambulance. The doctors said I was very lucky. They pumped my stomach and told me I'd almost died.

"And if that wasn't bad enough, the news made headlines in our local paper—'Local Musician Found Unconscious From Drug and Alcohol Overdose.' We were just getting ready to sign with a record company, but when they heard what had happened to me, they backed out. The guys were furious with me. They told me I either had to shape up or ship out.

"I'd 'hit bottom' as they say in AA. I'd almost killed myself, my wife and kids were gone, and I was very close to losing my band. I knew it was life or death for me. That's when I finally went to Alcoholics Anonymous.

"I can't tell you it was easy because it wasn't. It was damn hard. There were days when I didn't think I could make it without a drink. If I wasn't drinking, I didn't miss the drugs, but I sure missed the hooch—all the time. But I wanted to live and I knew I didn't have many chances left—if any."

Adrienne

At 30, Adrienne seemed to have it all. She was attractive and a highly successful executive for a large clothing chain. She had a handsome, adoring boyfriend and she owned a condo in West Los Angeles. Life was sweet. Then suddenly, she began to suffer from chronic fatigue.

"I always had so much energy, but suddenly I felt exhausted all the time," she said. "I had to force myself out of bed in the morning, and by midday, I had to lie down in my office to take a nap. I finally went to the doctor, but he couldn't find anything wrong with me. He didn't say it, but he implied that it might be psychosomatic.

"During the next year I became so weak I had to take a leave of absence from work. I went to doctor after doctor, but no one could discover the cause of my problem. Everyone I knew—my boyfriend, my friends, even my family—treated me like I had some kind of emotional problem, like I was making it up to get attention or something. It was so humiliating.

"My boyfriend finally broke up with me because he said he just couldn't stand seeing me suffer. But I know it was because I wasn't any fun anymore. Even my friends stopped calling. I never wanted to go anywhere, so I guess I don't blame them.

"I went to three other doctors before I finally found one who was able to determine what was wrong with me. He diagnosed me with chronic fatigue syndrome. He put me on a special diet and referred me to a woman who practices alternative medicine. After about two months on the diet and taking the special herbs she suggested, I finally started getting some of my energy back.

"The biggest blow was what happened once I returned

to work. My assistant had taken my place while I was out sick and I was very grateful to her. But when I came back, I noticed my bosses began to treat me like *I* was the assistant, giving me drudge work instead of the duties of an executive. When I complained, they made up excuses, telling me I'd been out of the loop so long that it would take time to get me back in. But as time went by it became clear that they had no intention of giving me my job back. And they were afraid to fire me because they knew I'd file suit against them."

A person with the second type of imbalance focuses too much attention on his body. As I mentioned earlier, this can be to the detriment of other aspects of someone's life, as it was with Rick.

Rick

Rick was a champion bodybuilder who had won several state and regional championships. The previous year he had come in second and third at the National Championship and was planning on taking first in the upcoming year. Unfortunately, Rick was disqualified from the competition and barred for life from the sport after officials discovered that he was using steroids.

"I was absolutely devastated. I'd worked so hard for so long to reach this level, and it was all taken away from me. I was furious because so many of the other guys use steroids, too, but they just didn't get caught. Why me? I thought. Why am I the one to have my entire life ruined like this?

"My whole life had been centered around making my body the best it could be. I studied nutrition, stress management, visualization and many other techniques to get my body in tip-top shape. Now it all felt hopeless. I became really depressed. I stopped working out and started eating anything I wanted.

"I gained about 50 pounds in less than two months. At that point I was ashamed to go out of the house for fear some of my buddies would see me."

As we saw with Rick, in this second type of imbalance there is often too much attention focused on the body's appearance. Until very recently, men have not had to suffer quite as much pressure regarding the way their bodies should look as women, but that is rapidly changing. Today men are constantly being pressured to work out, pump up their muscles and stay physically fit. The message that men get today is that all women prefer a man who is athletic and muscular, even though that is not always true. Many women prefer men who are slender, and some even prefer men who are overweight—the "bear" look. Some find muscular men threatening because they feel either physically or emotionally overwhelmed by them.

Some people are obsessed with keeping their bodies "perfect" in order to hide their addictions, insecurities or other problems. Those who are co-dependent or who tend to gain their sense of self-identity primarily through the admiration of others focus on their bodies and keep them looking good, not from a sense of loving their bodies or caring about themselves, but to attract partners.

Our bodies come in all shapes and sizes, no two being alike. Yet in spite of this, most of us carry an ideal image in our heads of what we *should* look like.

Unfortunately, this image is usually one that we can never reach—the image indelibly etched in our minds by the media of the perfectly shaped Adonis or beauty queen. We are never satisfied with how we look. If we are tall, we wish we were shorter; if we are short, we want to be taller. We become convinced that if our breasts or our penis were larger, our sexual insecurities would be over. We focus on our bad points instead of our good ones, and because of this we assume everyone else does the same thing when they look at us.

We can appreciate others' beauty even when they aren't "perfect" and can understand, at least intellectually, that everyone has different ideas of what beauty is. However, if we are critical of a certain part of our body, we assume everyone else is as well. Even when others disagree with our assessment of our body, we argue with them, assuming they are being polite or that they just haven't looked closely enough.

As you read about Jennifer, you will see how a preoccupation with the body's appearance can often be a symptom of a deeper problem.

Jennifer

For years, Jennifer went on crash diets, fad diets and so-called healthy diets. But mostly she used diuretics, laxatives and purging to maintain her slender figure. She'd heard all about the dangers of binging and purging, but she didn't feel it applied to her.

"I exercised every day, but I wasn't too extreme," Jennifer explains. "I took plenty of vitamins and drank lots of water, just like they tell you to. Those other women, those anorexics and bulimics, they didn't take care of their body——that's why they got sick."

But Jennifer was wrong. At age 33, she suffered a heart attack and almost died. The doctors told her it was caused by an irregular heartbeat that was a result of her chronic vomiting and laxative abuse.

One of the main reasons so many women like Jennifer perceive their bodies as problems is that we live in a culture that dictates that women must be beautiful to be worthwhile, and then sets up standards of female beauty that are not only impossible for most women to live up to, but are unhealthy as well.

Getting and staying thin have become major pastimes for women, consuming a significant amount of their time, energy and money. According to Judith Stein of the Fat Liberation Movement, the emphasis on thinness in our culture not only oppresses overweight women, it also serves as a form of social control for all women.

In addition to endangering your health, being preoccupied with your looks also continuously lowers your self-esteem. It is difficult to dislike your body or a specific part of your body and still like yourself.

You don't have to lose weight, gain weight, develop more muscle tone or have plastic surgery in order to feel good about your body. You don't have to change your body in order to love it. Instead, you can decide to accept, love and feel gratitude toward your body just the way it is.

Loving our bodies is a difficult task for many people, and it will take time to learn to do so. Eventually, with practice, you can begin to appreciate and enjoy your body's uniqueness.

Your body is what it is for a variety of reasons—heredity, environment, diet, exercise, your emotional state, age, illness, etc. Many people, instead of having compassion for themselves and what they and their bodies have had to endure in life, are critical of their bodies, feeling as Adrienne did that somehow their bodies betrayed them. But our bodies do not betray us. They are instead a direct reflection of who we are, based on where we have come from and what we have had to endure.

An Imbalance of Power

Unless you choose to do great things with it,
it makes no difference how much you are
rewarded, or how much power you have.

OPRAH WINFREY

Power can be seen as power with
rather than power over, and it can be used for
competence and cooperation, rather than
dominance and control.

ANNE L. BARSTOW

Not only does absolute power corrupt absolutely, it also destroys relationships, isolates people and produces tremendous stress. With power comes incredible responsibility—responsibility that can become a burden. And like those who are extremely successful or who have reached some degree of fame, the powerful are often targets for the envy and projection of others.

You've probably heard the sayings, "Pride goeth before a fall" and "The bigger they are, the harder they fall." These sayings have become axioms because they have proved throughout the years to be consistently true.

There are various reasons for this. It is often our need to be above everyone else, to be famous, rich or successful, that sets us up for a fall in the first place. We can't expect to go too far up on a pedestal without realizing that someone is going to want to shake us down, especially if we stepped over others to get there. Those who have a pompous need to control or dominate others are the very ones who get knocked down first because others can't tolerate their attitude.

Lewis Smedes talks about "pride of power" in his book, *Shame and Grace.*

> A person with pride of power believes that his power itself gives him the right to do anything with his power that he gets into his head to do. [1]

---

[1] Smedes, 149.

How do we prevent success from destroying us, and how do we pick up the pieces once it nearly has? An imbalance of power indicates that there needs to be a leveling or equalizing in a person's life. For example, one person may have more power in a relationship than another. Or some people can become so famous or rich that they become isolated from others. There may be no others whom they consider "equals" or who consider themselves equal to the rich and famous.

Another significant reason why the powerful so often fall is because they tend to buy into the public persona projected onto them by other people. Doctors are supposed to be all-knowing, therapists are supposed to have it all together, ministers are supposed to be pious. When we begin to believe these expectations, we become conceited, pompous, unreachable. Then we are in trouble. The following examples illustrate how such an imbalance of power can create a fall.

Adam

Adam is a highly skilled surgeon for a prestigious hospital in Los Angeles. During his 10 years at the hospital, he'd established himself as one of the best surgeons in his field. He was highly respected by his patients and his colleagues. But he wasn't very well liked.

"I just didn't have time to stand around and chat with people. I had important things to do," he told me. "I know that's why people thought I was a snob. It wasn't that I thought I was better than them; I just had better things to do."

As I got to know Adam, it became clear by the way he talked about people that he tended to be arrogant and rude, even cruel at times. "The nurses would get so snappy with me just because I expected them to do their jobs. They didn't like me ordering them around, but how else was I going to get them to do what I needed them to do? If they'd been smart enough to figure out what to do, I wouldn't have to yell at them. I told them that a hundred times."

Adam had come to me because he felt extremely enraged and humiliated when he wasn't chosen for chief of surgery, a position he had thought he had been guaranteed to win. He was told that although his work was superb, he didn't have good relationships with other staff members. In evaluations, several staff members complained of his incessant pressure for performance, his unawareness of their needs and his intolerance for mistakes. This took him completely by surprise.

After several weeks of therapy, more and more of the story unfolded.

"And then, to make matters worse, when I told my wife what happened, she complained that my relationship with her and with our children was just as bad. She complained that I'm never home, and that I'm cold and aloof when I am. She said I expect to be treated like a king just because I'm a famous surgeon and that I think my needs are more important than anyone else's in the family. I've never heard her talk like that. She sure had great timing."

Then to top it all off, the administration had chosen for chief of surgery a man that Adam despised. This felt like the ultimate slap in the face.

"I couldn't believe it when I heard that they'd chosen Jonathan Silverman. Jonathan Silverman is a wimp—a real butt kisser. That's why he got it. He doesn't know as much as I do. *No one* on that staff does. And no one has the reputation I do. I'm so angry, I don't know what to do. And now on top of everything else, there's this sexual harassment complaint."

Adam hadn't told me anything about this aspect of his problem until now. It turned out that there had been complaints filed against him by two nurses' aides and a receptionist. They accused him of touching them in inappropriate ways and making sexual comments about their bodies.

"I've never heard of anything so ridiculous in my life. Women fall all over themselves for me. I don't have to *force* women to have sex with me, for Christ's sake."

What Adam was to learn was that the women weren't complaining that he was "coming on" to them. They were upset because he made inappropriate, offensive comments about their bodies. Two of the women accused Adam of criticizing them for being overweight and slapping their butts in a derogatory manner. The other reported that he had made a comment about her breasts, asking her if she'd had a breast job. All three women said they had felt demeaned by his comments.

"No wonder they gave the position to Jonathan Silverman. They were afraid of scandal. They didn't want the hospital to look bad. They didn't even talk to me first—the cowards. All this sexual harassment garbage has gotten out of hand. I'm all for women's rights, but this is ridiculous. I didn't hurt those women."

As is typical of those who have power issues, Adam didn't have a clue about how his behavior and attitude affected others. It was going to take a long time for him to understand how he set himself up for his fall, and an even longer time to realize why.

William

William was required to seek counseling as part of his sentence for battering his wife. He made it very clear from the beginning that he resented being forced into therapy and insisted there was nothing wrong with him.

"I want you to know that this is a tremendous waste of time and money. I don't believe in therapy. I think you're all a bunch of crackpots who live off the vulnerability of weak people."

He denied having abused his wife. Instead of insisting that he admit he had a problem, which I was sure he wasn't ready to do, I asked him to tell me how his arrest had affected him.

"How do you think I felt? I was furious. They didn't have to handcuff me in front of the entire neighborhood! I wasn't a common criminal, for Christ's sake. I would have gone along quietly."

"What happened next?" I asked.

"What do you think happened next? They locked me up. Of course, I put up a bond and was released in a couple of hours, but it was humiliating being put into a cell with all the local drunks and petty thieves. I had to get out of there. I'm an important man. I have responsibilities. I have a company to run."

William made sure I understood that he was the owner of a large manufacturing company and that he was worth millions.

"That's why Emily's doing this, you know. She thinks if she accuses me of battery, she'll get more money in the divorce settlement. But she's got a surprise coming. I'm hiring one of the world's best-known divorce attorneys. She's going to be sorry she messed with me."

I pressed him to tell me what had happened the night of his arrest.

"We were having a fight, that's all. The same fight we have all the time. Emily was complaining that I didn't spend enough time at home, and I was telling her she was lucky I came home at all, that if she hadn't gotten so fat I might have something to come home to. She lost it and started screaming, so I had to shut her up. After all, I didn't want the neighbors to hear."

"What do you mean, 'shut her up'?" I asked.

"Oh, I just slapped her in the face a little. She was hysterical."

"And what happened after that?"

"Well, things just got out of hand. She slapped me back, and I had to push her away to keep her from really hurting me. She hit her head against the wall. I went over to help her and then she went crazy—hitting and kicking. She told the police that the bruises all over her body were from me hitting her, but she caused most of those bruises herself. I was just trying to protect myself."

It was clear to me that William was in very deep denial. My only hope was that in time he'd come to trust me enough to let his defenses down and admit he had a problem.

As I discussed in my book *The Emotionally Abused Woman,* an important element in nearly all emotionally and physically abusive relationships is an inequality of power. This is often brought about because one person feels superior to the other. When one person is *devalued* and the other is *idealized,* the idealized one feels entitled to preferential treatment, which can lead to a controller mentality.

Any good relationship is necessarily a relationship of equals. This means that both parties contribute equally to the relationship, and that each is seen as an equal in the other's eyes. For example, while one person may contribute more money to the relationship, the other may contribute more time and energy maintaining the home and taking care of children. One may be more secure socially, while the other may contribute by being wiser with money. What is important is that each partner recognize and *value* the contributions made by the other.

If you suspect there is an inequality of power in your relationships, and that this may reflect a general imbalance of power in your life, the following questions will help you spot any inequality that exists. Take some time to give serious consideration to the questions before answering them. You may wish to have your partner, friends or coworkers answer the questions as well.

1. Who has more personal power in the relationship? That is, who seems to be the stronger of the two, in terms of being able to ask for what he or she wants and being able to take care of himself or herself emotionally?
2. Which one of you has a stronger need to be in control? Who usually gets his or her way in terms of choosing what the two of you will do at any given time? If you are in an intimate relationship, who has control over the finances? Who is more in control of your sexual relationship?
3. Which one of you seems to be less satisfied with your partner and with the relationship? Which one

has more complaints about not getting his or her needs met in the relationship? Which of you is more critical of the other?

4. Which person has more self-confidence? Which one feels better about himself or herself?

5. Which of you is more successful in his or her career? Who makes more money?

6. Do you think that one of you loves (or likes) the other more? Who is more emotionally dependent on the other? Which one of you would have a harder time going on without the other one?

7. Would you say one of you feels superior to the other one in the relationship? If so, why?

If you've answered "me" to most of these questions, you have more power in the relationship than your partner, friend or coworker. It is abusive of you to use this power to control your mate, friend or coworker. If you feel you have done so, or if you strongly identified with either Adam or William, your fall was probably caused by an imbalance of power.

An Imbalance of "Goodness"

Be aware that a halo has to fall only
a few inches to be a noose.

DAN MCKINNON

The most common and most significant type of imbalance is that caused by attempting to be "all good." Those who try to be *all* things to *all* people, to be kind at *all* costs, and whose focus in life is to save the world, especially when it means ignoring their own needs, almost inevitably fall. This is because there really is no such thing as an "all good" person. The very nature of being human is to be both good and bad.

We are all a combination of good and bad qualities; we all share the capacity to do both good and evil.

Ironically, it is those who stand out as the *most* moral, the *most* kind and the *most* magnanimous who are the *most* likely to fall. It is a rule of nature that the higher up on the pedestal we allow others to put us, the farther we have to fall. The more devout, respectable and altruistic we seem to be in the eyes of others, the more likely it is that we have a dark side just waiting to get out.

As humans, we contain within ourselves a whole spectrum of urges and potential behavior, but society, religion and our parents reinforce some and discourage others. While it is important for children to learn certain social behaviors in the process of growing up, the very act of encouraging some while discouraging others creates within us all a *shadow* personality. These rejected qualities do not cease to exist simply because they've been denied direct expression. Instead, they live on within us and form the secondary personality that psychology calls the Shadow.

Thus, there is a part we hide away not only from others but from ourselves. This dark side is made up of forbidden thoughts and feelings, undesirable and thus rejected personality traits, and all the violent and sexual tendencies we consider evil, dangerous or forbidden.

Sometimes we are aware of our dark side, and out of fear of being propelled into acting in ways that we will regret, we consciously work at subduing and controlling our more prurient or unacceptable urges. More often, though, we are entirely unaware of it. But our dark side, if hidden long enough, will eventually take over our personality in some unforeseen way and cause us to act in ways that would normally appall us. The more we suppress our so-called bad tendencies, the bigger, stronger and darker they become, until finally—either as an act of weakness or rebellion—we do something very bad. We then usually overcompensate by being extremely good, and the cycle starts all over again.

Jim

This was the case with Jim, a devoted father and husband who entered therapy after doing something he felt was so abhorrent that it rocked him to his very soul.

Jim spent all his free time with his wife and children. This was in sharp contrast to his own father, who had spent most evenings at the neighborhood bar carousing with other women while Jim was growing up. Unconsciously, Jim vowed to be as different from his father as he could possibly be.

But had Jim been more aware of himself, he would have known that there were needs inside of him that weren't being met—for time alone, for the companionship of friends, for the freedom to shed some of the responsibilities he took on so willingly. Because he suppressed these needs, they festered. Over time, a beast grew within Jim that became more and more restless.

The situation came to a head when his company sent him to a weekend convention. Finally away from home and his wife and children, Jim cut loose. His dark side, well-hidden for so long, completely took over. The first night he drank too much, partied too much and stayed up all night.

A little embarrassed the next day, he decided to take it easy that night and go to bed early. But from the moment he downed his first cocktail early in the evening, he was headed for disaster. Unaccustomed to drinking, "quiet, responsible" Jim suddenly became loud, reckless and the life of the party.

When he woke up the next morning he had little recollection of the night before. To his horror, he found two prostitutes in bed with him and cocaine and drug paraphernalia on the coffee table. Although he was extremely hung over, he managed to get the women up, dressed and out of his room before collapsing back in bed.

When he woke up again, the telephone was ringing incessantly. His wife was on the line, demanding to know what was going on. Startled, Jim asked what she meant. Extremely upset, his wife informed him that he had called her at 2:30 A.M. to tell her that he was having a wonderful time without her. Then he had hung up. When she tried to call him back, a woman answered the phone and said above the din of loud music and laughter that Jim was busy.

Jim couldn't believe what he was hearing, but the bad news didn't end there. He discovered that he had blown nearly $3,000 on the prostitutes and the drugs. Worse yet, until he was tested, he was worried sick that he had also contracted AIDS.

Those employed in the helping professions are particularly vulnerable to a fall. This is true for several reasons. First of all, their choice of profession often reflects a strong and abiding need to be seen as "good." Helping others often becomes their primary way of gaining approval and love from others and of boosting their self-esteem. In addition, they often sacrifice themselves for others to the point of losing all sense of right and wrong, and they often begin to identify with the persona projected upon them by others. This was the case with Marion.

Marion

Marion was a highly respected psychologist who cared deeply about her clients. She constantly sought to improve her skills so that she could be the best therapist possible. She was also dedicated to improving the overall level of competency of all psychologists, and to this end became a member of the ethics committee of the board of the American Psychological Association (APA). A strong advocate for clients' rights, Marion worked to strengthen the rules concerning dual relationships between therapist and client (therapists having a personal or business relationship with a client outside of therapy).

But all this was before she became attracted to one of her clients. Putting her beliefs aside, Marion rationalized that she and her patient were an exception to the rule—they were truly in love and deserved to be together. Although she had been extremely critical of male therapists who have sex with their patients, she felt her situation was entirely different because no sex occurred in her office. Instead, she terminated her therapeutic relationship with her patient and set out to wait the then-required period of six months before beginning a romantic relationship with him.

But Marion was unable to wait and instead began a torrid affair with her ex-patient only two months after the therapist/patient relationship ended. When she left him 10 months later, her lover, in an act of revenge, reported her to the APA. Her reputation in the psychological community was ruined, and eventually her license to practice was revoked.

Society sets certain people up to be "good." Ministers, priests, nuns and other religious leaders are expected to have exemplary characters, to always put the needs of others before their own, and to dedicate themselves to goodness. Father Patrick Murphy is a prime example of this.

Father Murphy

Father Murphy was highly respected and deeply loved by his parishioners. He had been at the same parish for five years and was treated like a member of the family by many of his parishioners. He frequently had dinner with them and attended their parties. And so, when an altar boy accused Father Murphy of sexually molesting him, no one could believe it.

Unfortunately, it was the truth. Although he initially denied it, when his bishop asked him directly whether he had done it, he finally confessed.

"I was actually relieved to have it out in the open," said Father Murphy. "I knew I had a problem, but I just couldn't seem to stop on my own. I knew I needed to be stopped. I had put it in God's hands, and I now believe this was his answer."

His parishioners were, of course, devastated. They felt deeply disappointed and betrayed. Certainly the sexual abuse of a child is a horrible crime against God and man. But for a priest to commit this kind of atrocity was doubly horrific. Or was it? Wasn't Father Murphy human, after all, with the same weaknesses, human frailties and problems that we all have? Why does the fact that he was a priest make us expect more of him than we do others?

An Imbalance
of the Soul

As Thomas Moore writes in *Care of the Soul,*

> Loss of soul is the great malady of the 20th century.
> When soul is neglected, it doesn't just go away; it appears symptomatically in obsessions, addictions, violence, and loss of meaning. Our temptation is to isolate these symptoms or to try to eradicate them one by one; but the root problem is that we have lost our wisdom about the soul, even our interest in it. [1]

What is soul? It has to do with depth and genuineness, as when we say certain music has soul or that a

---

[1] Thomas Moore, *Care of the Soul: A Guide for Cultivating Depth and Sacredness in Everyday Life.* (New York: HarperCollins, 1992), xi.

remarkable person is soulful. It has to do with experiences that stay in the memory and touch the heart—
experiences like connecting with nature or connecting
deeply with another person. According to Moore, soul
lies midway between unconsciousness and understanding, and its instrument is neither the mind nor the body,
but the imagination. Those who experience a fall are
often disconnected from their soul, some more than
others. Those whose souls are most deprived do not
feed their soul what it desperately needs—beauty, creativity, solitude, nature. They do not take the time to
feed their soul art, music, literature and beautiful scenes
from nature, but instead feed it a steady diet of concrete
and steel, noise and television.

For some, an imbalance of the soul means that they
have lost contact with a higher purpose or a higher
power. They may have become so busy in their lives that
they have stopped spending time connecting with their
soul and with their creator. There is indeed a strong connection between spirituality and soul. More and more we
are finding that a spiritual life of some kind is absolutely
necessary for emotional health.

Because many people do not believe in the soul or
have lost contact with their soul, we give it little or no
value in our hierarchy of values. As Moore eloquently
states, "We have come to know soul only in its complaints: when it stirs, disturbed by neglect and abuse, and
causes us to feel its pain." [2]

---

[2] Moore, xiii.

Teri

Teri began treatment with me because she was extremely depressed over her husband leaving her. When I asked her why she thought he left, she feigned innocence, saying she didn't really know. But after a few sessions, she admitted to me that he left because she had refused to get help for her problem. She was a compulsive shopper. Within two years, they were more than $40,000 in credit-card debt and had to file for bankruptcy.

"We almost lost our house because we'd taken out a second mortgage in order to pay off some of the bills I'd racked up," Teri agonized.

When I asked her why she hadn't tried to get help earlier, as her husband had requested, she explained that she thought she could do it on her own. It took her husband leaving to bring her to her senses and force her to admit she needed help.

During her therapy, Teri uncovered a great deal about her past, which helped to explain her current behavior.

"I grew up in a very poor home where there was very little intellectual or emotional stimulation," she explained. "My parents were uneducated, and there wasn't a lot of love between them. I know they loved us, but they were always so busy working, they didn't have time to spend with us. I can best describe my childhood as barren, gray, boring. It was always the same routine every day: school, then home to take care of my little brother and to cook dinner for the family. During the summer I was expected to take care of Robbie and clean the house while my parents were at work, and to have their dinner ready for them when they got home. I didn't really have a childhood."

Teri grew up feeling empty inside. "I don't think I ever saw my parents laugh or play around with each other. Everything was so serious. It was like life was just a struggle, no joy, no fun."

And then Teri met her husband, Carl. She was attracted to his sunny disposition and his wisecracking ways. "He made me laugh and he didn't take life so seriously. I fell in love with him right away. I wanted to be around him because he made me feel so good."

But after they were married, started having children and bought their first home, Carl became much more serious.

"There were bills to pay and Carl worked hard in construction. When he got home, all he wanted to do was sit in front of the TV and drink his beer. Pretty soon we hardly talked to one another, much less had any fun together."

For a time Teri immersed herself in taking care of their two children, Tammy and Stevie. She loved them both very much, but was becoming increasingly depressed staying home and taking care of them. She'd planned to go to college after she and Carl were married, but she became pregnant right away with Tammy and her academic plans were put on hold.

"That's when I first started my compulsive shopping," Teri admitted. "I started by spending too much on toys and clothes for the kids. Carl complained a little, but he wanted to spoil them too, so he didn't say all that much. But then I got more and more carried away. I started buying things for the house, for the yard, clothes for myself. Eventually I was buying things we didn't even need. Carl was becoming more and more upset, and I knew I had to stop, but somehow I just couldn't."

What Teri came to realize was that shopping gave her the excitement and stimulation she longed for so desperately.

Buying something gave her a temporary feeling of stimulation, pleasure and contentment she'd found no other way. She was suffering from emotional and spiritual deprivation.

Another example of an imbalance of the soul is the addict or alcoholic, who, in addition to suffering from an addictive personality, can often suffer from other problems. While alcoholism is a disease that is often inherited and is not caused by a lack of will or character, many alcoholics do suffer from an imbalance of the soul, as was the case with Jack.

Jack

Jack had loved to party since he was a teenager. He loved going out to dance and drink with his friends and was often the life of the party. He was outgoing, funny and well-liked by many people. But as the years went by and many of his friends started settling down into their careers and marriages, Jack kept partying. He worked hard during the day as a defense attorney, but after work he hit the bars. His friends marveled at how he had the stamina to go out almost every night and still work as hard as he did. He was a relentless, hard-hitting lawyer who won almost all his cases. By age 33 he was up for full partnership in his firm.

But in spite of his success, things started falling apart for Jack. Although women loved his charm and sexiness, he was known as a womanizer who found it impossible to be faithful, no matter how much he liked a particular woman. And increasingly, his drinking was beginning to interfere with his work. He found it harder and harder to get up in the morning, and several times he missed court dates with clients.

Jack's fall from grace finally came when he got behind the wheel intoxicated late one night and broadsided a taxi cab. Both the driver and one of the passengers in the cab were seriously injured. Jack was arrested for drunk driving and reckless endangerment.

Jack had broken the morals clause in his contract with his law firm, which didn't want the adverse publicity, so he was asked to leave. And although he hired one of the best criminal attorneys available, he was convicted and given a jail sentence of six months, with five years of probation.

At this point you have probably discovered that an imbalance in one or more areas of your life contributed to, if not created, your fall. Whether your fall is a physical, emotional or spiritual one, the discovery of this imbalance can be the biggest blessing of all because now you have the unique opportunity to right that imbalance, round out your personality, become a healthier person, and create a new life that is more harmonious and balanced. In the next section, you will see how some of the people you have met so far went about doing just that, and discover the blessings that came from their endeavors.

PART III

BLESSINGS FROM THE FALL

> Throughout my life, I have
> always found that events which seemed at
> the time disastrous ultimately developed into
> positive blessings. In fact, I have never
> known one instance when this was
> not proved to be the case.
>
> ELISABETH MARBURY

Unfortunately, for many of us, it takes a fall from grace to break through our thick barriers of defensiveness, ego, pride, selfishness and greed. A fall can bring us down to earth long enough to smell the roses, hug the trees, connect with our bodies and souls, and discover what is really important in life.

Experiencing a fall from grace can create an internal environment that forces us to make profound changes, changes we might never have made any other way. It is often only through such a fall that we can come to know our true selves, come to face things about ourselves that we might never have faced, discover aspects of ourselves that might have remained otherwise hidden from us. These newly discovered aspects can round out our character, add depth to our emotions, provide us with new avenues of creativity, and help us connect with others and learn further insights into ourselves.

My thesis is that a fall from grace is first and foremost a wake-up call, our creator's way of getting our attention, shaking us up, teaching us a lesson. That lesson may be to make us painfully aware of the imbalances in our lives, or a warning intended to prevent us from causing more harm to ourselves or others. For example, people who lose their licenses because of driving drunk may have avoided killing themselves or someone else.

There are other benefits as well. A fall from grace can also offer:

- A chance to reevaluate or review your life, take stock, and view your fall as your own near-death experience because that is, in essence, what it is
- A reminder that you have unfinished business to deal with from your past or an opportunity to discover your true self
- A test of your faith, or a chance to prepare for something important

In the following chapters I will show how all the people you have met so far were able to find the blessings in their fall. I will also share with you my experience, and how my fall helped me to lower my defenses, face the truth about my own damage, work on being nonjudgmental and face my narcissism.

A Question
of Balance

I have been sick and I found out, only then, how
lonely I am. Is it too late?

EUDORA WELTY

"To balance" means to bring into harmony or proportion. If you focus all your attention on one
person or one area of your life to the detriment
of others, you will have nothing to fall back on if that
part of your life becomes troubled or that relationship
doesn't last. A healthier way to live is to lead a balanced
life, involving your whole self: body, mind and spirit. A

healthy person tries to create harmony between these three aspects of their life by focusing attention on each and by not sacrificing one for the others.

For example, this may mean getting to know your body for the first time, or making an important mind/body connection. It may mean exploring the different aspects of soul and spirit, reconnecting with your higher power or with nature.

In this chapter you will see how many of the people you have met so far went about creating more equilibrium and stability in their lives. I will also make suggestions as to how you can create more balance in your own life.

Rick

You will remember Rick from the previous section on the imbalance of the body. When I met Rick, he was grossly overweight and extremely depressed. He'd come into therapy at the urging of a close friend who was also seeing me.

"I don't know what you can do for me," he said. "I don't think anyone can help."

"It sounds like you've given up hope," I ventured.

"Yeah, the way I see it, I blew my chance for a happy life. End of story."

As Rick filled me in on what had happened to him, I was amazed at the extent of his denial. While he explained how important keeping his body in tip-top shape had been, he didn't recognize the dangers of steroids. When I confronted him about this seeming contradiction, he became very defensive.

"Oh, I don't believe all that crap," he countered. "There really isn't any proof that steroids cause health problems. It's all a bunch of lies aimed at getting people to stop. The fact is, most bodybuilders use them and lots of other athletes, too, and they're all fine."

By the end of the first session, Rick was at least able to talk about how disgusted he was that he'd gained so much weight. "I hate my body now. You wouldn't believe how good I looked before. But now all those muscles have just turned into fat. I'd like to work on getting my motivation and willpower back."

I explained to Rick that before that could happen, we needed to help him work through his depression and create more balance in his life. He agreed to try.

The next week he reported that just getting out of the house to come into therapy had helped him a little. "At least I'm not lying around, obsessing about missing the championship that's coming up. And it does feel good to have someone to talk to."

I asked Rick if he had any other interests except bodybuilding and how he was supporting himself since he wasn't working. He explained that he was living off money his parents had put aside for his college education. When he became serious about bodybuilding, his enthusiasm helped to convince them to give him the money to pay for his training.

Clearly Rick had suffered from both an imbalance of the body and the heart since he'd invested his entire being in becoming a bodybuilding champion. The first thing we needed to do was to help him connect with other parts of himself—his soul, his emotions and his mind.

This was not going to be easy. Rick explained that he'd been a jock in school and had taken little interest in any of his academic classes. He'd only graduated high school because he was such a credit to the school as a star athlete. And although he'd gone out with lots of girls in high school, he hadn't dated much since then because he was so focused on bodybuilding.

"I just didn't want to take the time," Rick explained. "I didn't want to stay out late at night and I sure didn't want to drink and party too much. It just wasn't worth it."

Now he felt so embarrassed by his body that he refused to even consider dating.

"Are you kidding? No girl is going to go out with me in *this* condition."

Clearly it was going to be a real challenge to get Rick interested in anything other than bodybuilding. But eventually we hit pay dirt. It turned out that Rick had always had a secret desire to design and create women's fashions. It was understandable that he had kept this interest a secret. The image of this big bruiser sewing women's clothing was quite a humorous one.

"Can you just see it? Me with a needle and thread in my hand, prancing around fitting clothes on models?"

But I was elated that we'd found another interest, an artistic one at that. Art is an extraordinary way to connect with one's soul and to help a person express emotions he could never reveal any other way.

With a little encouragement, Rick enrolled in a few beginning art courses at a local junior college. The next semester he enrolled as a full-time student in the art program and was taking both a clothing design and a textiles course. In the meantime, he began designing his own creations.

"I never thought I'd ever want to do anything as much as bodybuilding. But I *love* creating my own designs. I'm using a part of myself I wasn't even in touch with before—

my creativity. It's opened up amazing possibilities for me. I love going to art openings and museums and seeing what other artists are doing. Artists are very interesting people, you know?"

I was glad to hear that in addition to finding another passion, Rick was also socializing. But there was still imbalance in Rick's life. While his extra weight was coming off from all the added activity, he was still eating unhealthy food and wasn't exercising at all. It seemed that he was still suffering from "sour grapes." If he couldn't be a champion bodybuilder, he wasn't going to pay attention to his body at all. He had merely traded one body imbalance for another.

I worked with Rick to help him to appreciate his body for the things it provided him. I encouraged him to appreciate his hands for the wonderful things they helped him create and for their ability to help him feel different textures, his eyes for helping him to see beautiful colors and designs. Ever so slowly, Rick began to connect with his body in a very different way than he had ever done before.

I explained to Rick that it was important that he begin to accept every part of himself. Our bodies are vehicles that carry us where we want to go, provide for us a great deal of physical and sensory pleasure, house our brains and vital organs and provide for the very breath of life. Instead of focusing on the imperfect parts of our body, we must begin to accept our body as an inextricable part of ourselves.

"You know, it's funny," Rick said. "I was so focused on building up my muscles, on the *esthetics* of the way my body looked, that I didn't really appreciate the finer aspects of what the body does for us. I thought I was connected to my body, but I wasn't. And I sure didn't appreciate it like I do now."

Rick had created balance in his life. He was connected to his mind, his body and his soul, and he understood the importance of not focusing on only one aspect of his life to the exclusion of the rest. It was time for Rick to stop therapy and try making it on his own.

Teri

Teri is the woman I wrote about earlier who entered therapy because her husband had left her due to her problems with compulsive shopping. After several sessions, Teri shared this with me:

"After Carl left, I was forced to take a good long look at myself. I'd often blamed him for my feelings of boredom and discontent, his refusal to move from that chair once he got home, or to carry on an adult conversation with me. But once I was alone, I realized I was still bored. The kids were at school every day and after school they were of an age where they spent little time at home. Shopping had become my only outlet, my only reason for getting out of the house, my only form of stimulation."

My first suggestion to Teri was to check out a 12-Step program for compulsive spenders called Debtors Anonymous. There she found that she wasn't alone with her problem and acquired some important tools to help stop her compulsive spending.

But Teri also needed to work on discovering who she was, what her preferences were and what kinds of interests she had, something many people are fortunate enough to be able to do as they grow up, particularly during their adolescence. But since Teri had been raised in an emotional and cultural vacuum, she hadn't been afforded this exploratory period.

With my encouragement, Teri set out in the world on a mission of discovery. Instead of going to the malls, I suggested she go to art galleries, to museums, to botanical gardens and on nature walks. I encouraged her to go to movies and plays in the evening, instead of sitting in front of the television. After only a month of this kind of exploration, Teri told me excitedly: "There's a whole world out there I never even knew existed. I feel like a kid in a candy store. There's so much to see and do and learn about. It's so exciting."

Outside of therapy, Teri was discovering the world and filling her soul with music, art and nature. Inside therapy, she was filling herself up with her feelings. She'd never been given permission by her parents to express her emotions, and so an important part of her therapy was for her to begin to feel free to acknowledge and express the feelings she normally kept hidden from others and even herself.

In one breakthrough session Teri explained, "I love Carl, but he's become just like my parents, never expressing his feelings, never talking to me. And he always communicated the message to me, just like they did, that my emotions are too intense, that I am supersensitive. Part of my compulsive shopping was my way of getting back at him for treating me just like my parents did."

With the help of therapy and Debtors Anonymous, Teri recovered from her compulsive spending in only a few months. It took somewhat longer for her to reconnect with her emotions and her soul. During her time of exploration she discovered she had an interest in and aptitude for botany. "I feel my best when I'm around plants. I love learning about them, which ones have healing qualities, which ones are drought-resistant."

Teri eventually got a job in a nursery and now volunteers her time as a docent for a botanical garden in her area. She's also entered college to study to become a botanist.

The Riches of the Dark Side

Another balance we must strive for in our lives is that between the so-called "good" and "bad" sides of ourselves. Like Jim, Marion and Father Murphy, many people go through life bent on being good. Detached from their dark side, they are also detached from the wonderful things the dark side offers us—passion, depth, creativity, sensuous pleasures and a sense of humor.

When we disown our dark side, we are indeed less alive, less spirited. A rich vitality lies bottled up beneath our acceptable personality. By discovering and owning our dark side, we get in touch with this life energy. Only by finding and redeeming those wishes and traits that we chronically deny in ourselves can we move toward wholeness and healing.

But how do we meet the Shadow? By conceding that there are parts of ourselves that we abhor, despise or deny; by acknowledging those parts, no matter how horrific they are; and by seeing that we are still ourselves. To acknowledge a part of our self that is both stranger and kin is to enter into one of the greatest mysteries of the psyche. This act in itself becomes a peace offering that encourages the Shadow to emerge.

The medical model of immunization offers a parallel to this process. When we are immunized against disease, our bodies know instinctively how to make good use of a poison or disease-producing substance that in larger amounts would harm us. The ability to admit the Shadow, to allow it into consciousness in manageable doses, similarly allows us to immunize the psyche.

It is a paradox of consciousness that allowing and admitting the Shadow reduces its power, producing the opposite of what we feared. By making ourselves vulnerable to it, we achieve an immunity to its deadliness. Instead of being overwhelmed by our darker urges, we learn to coexist with them; we can nod knowingly when they appear, gratefully take the lessons they give us and turn these lessons into healthy emotional or creative expression. I've seen time and again in my practice that recognizing the dark side produces a powerful and beneficial change in consciousness.

For example, Charles, who was impotent in response to his urge to rape someone as he had been raped as a child, regained his sexuality once he was able to express his rage concerning his own victimization.

Susan, who almost lost her medical license because of her incompetence, learned that she was hiding behind her persona as "healer" and ignoring her own serious drinking problem.

Philip, a long-time minister whose affair with a married female parishioner was discovered by his congregation, learned true humility and compassion for sinners after years of feeling superior to his congregants.

Our dark side is a gold mine of depth, mystery, richness, substance, knowledge, creativity, insight and power. According to Carl Jung, the dark side is 90 percent gold. But unless we can mine those riches, we are presenting to the world and to ourselves only half a person. Exploring and owning our dark sides make us whole and transform us, not into monsters, but into more empathetic, less judgmental *human* beings.

In the following three examples, you will learn of the benefits reaped by Marion, Jim and Michele when they faced their dark sides and realized that they no longer had to strive to be good all the time.

Marion

Marion is the psychologist I discussed earlier who had an affair with a client. Although losing her license was devastating, it forced her to face certain issues in her life that she might never have faced any other way. "I was busy helping others and trying to impact the system, but I was neglecting my own psyche," said Marion. "I hadn't been in therapy in years and was convinced that I no longer needed to work on myself. I told myself I was fine, and most of the time I felt I was. It made me feel good when I worked with clients, and I was able to push down any problems I had by focusing on theirs.

"But I was really a lonely woman who didn't open up to anyone, not even the few close friends I had. I hadn't been in a relationship with a man in years. I'd convinced myself I was past all that, that I didn't need a man in my life to be happy. Be that as it may, I was denying the loneliness I felt deep inside. Because I saw so many clients almost every day, it felt like I had all the contact with people I needed.

"After I became involved with a client I was forced to face the fact that I *was* lonely. And I had to face the fact that I needed to get myself back into therapy to resolve some old issues."

When Marion started therapy with me she felt extremely vulnerable. It is often difficult for therapists to seek help themselves. But her fall had caused her to lower her defenses enough to admit she needed my help. Telling me about her affair with a client was the most difficult part, but once it was out in the open she progressed at a rapid speed.

Artwork was one of the tools Marion used to express her pent-up emotions. She worked on huge oil paintings, vibrant in color and emotion. Through painting she discovered a freedom and joy she'd never felt before. Today her paintings sell well enough for her to make a living solely on her art.

More important, she says: "Had I not had my fall, I would have gone on for years, sitting for hours listening to the problems of others and avoiding my own. Before, I was always tired, and now I realize it was because I was depressed. Now I look forward to every new day because I'm doing what I really want to do. I never would have found painting if I hadn't used it initially to voice my pain and shame over my fall and eventually to express my dark side."

Through art Marion began a whole new career, found expression to her repressed and suppressed emotions, and also became more connected with others.

"My art touches people in a way that my work as a therapist never did. And I find that although I spend many hours alone with my painting, I am aware that I need human contact as well. I've joined several artists' organizations and I socialize far more than ever. I still haven't found a partner, but now that I've worked through more of my issues concerning intimacy, I find I am more open to men. I even have a few male friends, and I'm hopeful that I may meet a man I want to become romantically involved with."

Jim

Jim entered therapy with me in order to understand what caused him to become so reckless with his marriage, his reputation and his very life.

Most of us are familiar with the old saying that it's what we don't know that can hurt us. Once we are aware of our dark side, we can exercise real control of it: not by suppressing it, but by respecting it, finding constructive outlets for it and setting limits.

When Jim began to explore his dark side in therapy, he found that he had tried so hard to be the opposite of his father that his normal, healthy need to have time away from his family had become transformed into Shadow material. His need to be *all good* had caused him to be only half a person. When he was able to acknowledge the fact that he didn't always want to be around his family and that they sometimes got on his nerves, he stopped taking himself so seriously and regained his sense of humor. He suddenly began to have far more energy and was able to participate in sports and to bring a new vitality to all aspects of his life—including his sex life with his wife.

Falling from grace has more to do with being *disgraced* in the eyes of our peers than it does with being disgraced in the eyes of our creator. In spiritual terms, grace is God's acceptance of our whole self, both the so-called good and bad aspects, as Michele Pillar Carlton was to learn.

Michele Pillar Carlton

Michele discovered a lot about grace, balance and accepting our wholeness from her fall from grace. She writes:

" 'An imbalance is an abomination to the Lord.' Proverbs 11:1. Sounds pretty scary, doesn't it? The first time I read this in the Bible I thought to myself, 'I'd hate to know what God means by that statement!' It sounded to me like a god who pats people on the head when they are good and just might slap you across the face when you fail.

"Balance is something I didn't experience growing up. As a child I loved sleeping over at my girlfriend's house next door because she ate dinner at about six o'clock each night with her family at the table. My favorite part about being there was slipping into her bed and feeling a top sheet against my legs. I didn't have a top sheet at home. Diane's sheets were cool and comforting, and the way they were tucked tight around the mattress felt secure to me, like her house did.

"There was a calm methodical rhythm to the way she lived. At my house nothing was calm. In a split second my family could go from uninvolved to yelling and screaming over nothing or everything. Life in my house was a balancing *act* . . . not balanced.

"Now fast forward the clock eight years. I'm 17 years old and I've found myself at a revival meeting in a small Baptist church near my high school.

"I was attending this meeting with a friend from school who had spent the last three months carefully telling me about her faith in a god whom she said loved me very much. I couldn't relate to parts of her story, especially the 'caring father' part. It was a little too foreign to me. But I did feel the love she seemed to be celebrating and could see that she and her friends were more stable than most kids at school. So that night, at the pastor's prompting, I walked forward and asked this god whom they spoke of to please give me a new start.

"As the months passed by in my new faith, I did feel a love I'd never known before, but I still felt no balance. The roots of my childhood ran deep around my tender new faith, sometimes choking it out.

"I was still driven by wanting to please people and to be accepted, and by the shame that seemed to be chasing me. I wish someone at that little church would have explained to me that healing 17 years of living in hell takes time, even for God. But I'd been given the opposite impression, believing that all had been made new the instant I'd prayed that first prayer.

"I wondered what was wrong with me. Once again, I felt the inner conflict I had felt growing up. The conflict of living two different lives, one public and one private. Were my imbalances too great even for God to settle?

"The life I longed for seemed to be happening in the people around me, but just slightly out of my reach. They seemed comfortable in their roles as church-going Christians. So much of what I was hearing from the teachings at the church confused me and seemed unattainable.

"I began to feel as though I were acting, just as I had as a child. Smiling on the outside, crying on the inside: that's what I had always been good at. As a believer in God, this act felt worse to me than it ever had without him. It felt like putting on a wet bathing suit.

"I had walked this tightrope as a child and now as a Christian. Inside I was screaming for someone to lower the rope and let me down to solid balanced ground. I longed for predictable footing where I could even dare to take a bad step without crashing to the ground below. But because I wasn't ready and didn't know how to deal with the past, I just stayed up there.

"In fact, the rope was raised higher and higher during the next few years as I became one of this country's top Christian recording artists. So you know what I did? I jumped. In front of God, the church, the audiences, the record label, friends and family. I made some very deliberate personal decisions that I knew would be met with great disapproval. It was professional suicide, the likes of which I'd not done before or since.

"Because of the destruction my choices had left in my path most people walked away, and when the time came for me to share with my peers, coworkers and friends what I'd learned and how I'd healed, there was no one around to listen.

"In the rubble, I'd lost my platform, but God was there and he listened very carefully. As I cried tears of loss and relief, he was there to wipe each one. I think it was about then that I realized that I had a new inheritance with a father who would never leave me. I learned to listen to his still, small voice, no longer listening to the screaming turmoil I knew as a child.

"As more time passed, I realized that God never wanted me up on the tightrope to begin with. The greatest healing of all was forgiving my mother and father for everything. This could not have been done without God.

"Lastly, I came to understand what God means in Proverb 11:1. He only hates imbalances because they keep us from walking straight into his loving arms."

Unequal Relationships

Another way we create imbalance in our lives is by having unequal relationships.

William

William is the man I mentioned earlier who had been referred to me for battering his wife. Although he was only required by law to attend therapy sessions for six months, by that time he recognized that he had a problem and chose to continue with me. During the months that we had been working together he had learned to trust me, and realized that he was an extremely unhappy person. William eventually opened up about his childhood, one that was plagued with horrible fights between his parents.

William's father had physically abused his mother.

"I despised her for putting up with it," William told me. "She was so weak. She'd always tell us she was going to leave him. She'd make these big plans about how we were going to start another life without him, how our life was going to be so much better. But she never followed through. He'd come home and they'd make up. It made me sick every time I saw her kissing and hugging him after what he'd done. I lost all respect for her."

Even though William's reaction to his mother sounds distorted, it is typical of what often occurs when a male child witnesses his father being abusive to his mother. He blames his mother for letting it happen, instead of allowing himself to feel his anger at his father for being abusive. To understand this reaction, it is important to realize that parents are their children's most powerful role models. When children witness one parent controlling or abusing the other, they are being shown two distinctly different ways of interacting: one as a victim, the other as an aggressor. Males in particular need someone to look up to, to respect and honor, to emulate. That is why it is common for a male child in this situation to become a batterer himself. Since they feel they have only two choices, to become a victim like their mother, or an aggressor like their father, most males will choose the latter at all costs.

"I grew up thinking that in every relationship there was a victim and a victimizer. I sure as hell wasn't going to be a victim like my mother," William confessed one day. "In my house, males had all the power. Even my brother and I had more power than my mother. By the time we started high school, we were ordering her around like my father did. When I married Emily, I just treated her like I'd learned to treat my mother."

In addition, many victims of childhood abuse, especially males, cope with their abuse by using a form of denial called "identifying with the aggressor." When a young child refuses to acknowledge to himself that he is being victimized, but instead justifies or minimizes the behavior of the abuser, he will often grow up to be very much like the abuser, behaving in the same abusive ways.

Two years and a divorce later, William was a different man.

"I can't believe what a bully I was," he told me. "Not only with Emily, but with my kids and even with my employees. I thought the best way to earn someone's respect was by intimidation. But I was *so wrong*. My kids respect me a lot more today than they ever did. They know I'm going to be fair with them, not just force them to do whatever I want. The same is true for my employees. I've learned you have to give people respect and treat them like equals, not like slaves.

What William began to realize was that because he'd felt so powerless in his childhood, he had become power-hungry. When he was a kid, his father had all the power and his mother had none. He used to wonder what it felt like to order people around like his father did. As an adult, the more power he got, the more he wanted. It was a very heady experience to be able to tell people what to do and see them jump.

"I realize now that I married Emily because she seemed so weak and helpless. Being around her made me feel more powerful. I was able to feel much stronger than I really am. Unfortunately, I didn't realize that I would come to hate her for her weakness, just like I hated my mother for hers."

Fortunately, William began to realize that a healthy relationship is one of equals. As I mentioned earlier, this means that both parties contribute equally to the relationship and that each is seen as an equal in the other's eyes. An equal relationship is also one where there is a mutuality in decision-making and where both people take responsibility for themselves and do not blame the other for their problems.

A balanced life is one in which equal emphasis and energy is placed on body, mind and spirit; where both our "goodness" and our dark side are accepted, respected and embraced; and one in which we choose to have equal relationships with others, viewing ourselves as neither better nor worse than other people.

Wake-Up Calls: God's Way of Preparing You for Something

When one door shuts another opens.

SAMUEL PALMER

I began to have an idea of my life,
not as the slow shaping of achievement to fit
my preconceived purposes, but as the
gradual discovery and growth of a
purpose which I did not know.

JOANNA FIELD

In this chapter I will explain how a fall can be a wake-up call, a warning, God's way of getting your attention. As I mentioned earlier, if you are like me, you have to be hit over the head before you are willing to change. Falling from grace may have been God's way of shaking your shoulders, of finally getting your attention, forcing you to take heed of something in your life that desperately needed attention. For those who use this wake-up call or heed this warning, a tremendous transformation can take place. Others believe their fall was God's way of preparing them for something else to enter their lives.

Andrea

In Andrea's case, losing her job as a social worker turned out to be both a wake-up call and a preparation for something far more meaningful to enter her life.

"Timothy's death was a wake-up call, not only for me but for the city of Chicago," Andrea explained. "For years I'd been seeing so much pain that I had become numb to it. I'd lost hope that we as social workers could ever make a difference, and in some ways I was right. Changes need to be made on a higher level. New legislation needs to be passed in order to keep these kids out of their abusive homes. When Timothy died, people started complaining and insisting that something be done, and because of it some significant changes have begun.

"As for me, after months of depression I decided I wanted to help make those changes. First of all, I realized I'd needed the time off from my job. For years my entire existence was centered around my work, to the exclusion of everything else. When I was fired I was forced to discover a life outside of work. I remembered hearing that exercise can help lift depression, so I forced myself to take a walk every day. I was amazed at what I began to see. When I was working I never even noticed my surroundings. I was only focused on getting to work and back, getting from one client's house to the next. I began to pay attention to the poverty all around me, something I'd blocked out because it was too painful to see. I noticed the kids standing around on street corners instead of being in school, the derelicts lying on the ground, the hoodlums driving the streets. I decided I wanted to work for an agency that could do some good instead of one that just kept the status quo.

"I started looking for a job in agencies like the Red Cross, the Salvation Army, and even some Christian organizations. I'd never been a religious person and so I was surprised by my willingness to do this, but somehow it felt right. I don't think it was a coincidence that the one place that offered me a job was a Catholic Services agency. I took the job as assistant director of youth services, and it was the best thing that ever happened to me.

"In the three years since I've been here, I've been able to implement major changes in the structure of the organization. We've opened a youth center where poor children and adolescents from the neighborhood can come after school to study, play sports and receive counseling. We even have a tutoring program, and last year we had six computers donated to the center.

"Now, instead of abuse and poverty, I see real hope. I know we are making a difference in these kids' lives. I see it every day. Kids who would normally be out on the street are now making something of their lives. Many of our kids are going on to college with scholarships.

"My entire outlook on life has changed. I don't need to drink to numb my pain any longer, and I make sure I have a life outside the agency. And I take a vacation every year to really get away from it all. I have more friends than I've ever had in my life, and I've even started dating again.

"Most important, I have faith in God once again. It's ironic, me working for a Catholic organization, because I'm not Catholic. But I do believe in God and I don't think it matters what church you belong to as long as you're connected to God's love. Deep in my heart I really do believe God led me here and that losing my job was God's way of preparing me to do the work I'm doing today."

Jack

Jack's arrest for drunk driving and reckless endangerment and the subsequent loss of his job was certainly a wake-up call, but as in Andrea's case, it also caused him to realize he needed far more meaning in his life than his job was providing.

"After the accident and my arrest, I thought my career was ruined," said Jack. "I now have a felony on my record, and spending six months in jail sure wasn't easy. But it ended up being the best thing that ever happened to me—after I got through all the humiliation and guilt.

"I was forced to go to AA and I discovered I am an alcoholic. I celebrated my third year of sobriety last week. But equally important, I discovered that I was suffering from a sickness of the soul. In spite of the fact that I seemed to be a happy-go-lucky type guy, the life of the party, I was deeply unhappy. Life held no meaning for me. I was lost.

"After I got sober I came to realize that I hated my work. I never wanted to be a lawyer in the first place, but I had gone to law school because my dad wanted it so much. I tried my best to get into it, and for a while I convinced myself that I could really do some good being an attorney. But I ended up defending people I knew were guilty, and I hated it. And I hated the depths to which defense attorneys will sink in order to get their clients off.

"I was probably an alcoholic from the time I was a teenager. I mean, I think I inherited the 'alcohol gene,' if there is such a thing. But I was basically a social drinker for years. Eventually, though, I became so unhappy with my job that I really tried to drown my sorrows in the booze.

"Being in jail for six months made me realize that I didn't want to continue defending guilty people. You wouldn't believe the things I've heard in there. Most of those guys have committed far more crimes than they've been arrested for, and a lot of them have gone free on technicalities. I decided that when I got out, I was going to go to work for the D.A.'s office instead of working as a defense attorney—to try to put some of these guys behind bars for good.

"Most important, though, is that I realized I want to make a real difference in the world. I've been working on getting more AA programs set up in prisons, and I've been working on getting more public awareness about the dangers of drunk driving. I've set up an outreach program for young people and first-time offenders in my area to get them into counseling. All this has given my life meaning and purpose."

If Jack had not been arrested for drunk driving, he could have ended up killing someone or himself. Often a fall from grace can save our relationships and even our life or the lives of others. In Micky's case, becoming so ill from abusing his body saved his life; becoming clean and sober saved his relationship.

Micky

"AA and NA [Narcotics Anonymous] saved my life. I firmly believe that if it hadn't been for the support and encouragement I received at those meetings, I would have died from alcohol and drugs. I was one of the lucky ones. There are a lot of musicians I've known who haven't been so fortunate. I believe that God had been trying to get my attention for a long time, and that he'd given me several warnings. Thank goodness I finally heeded them.

"I was in AA and NA for four months before Carrie finally believed I was serious about staying clean and sober and moved back home with the kids. Once we started talking again, she told me how close she'd been to leaving several times before because of how I'd act when I was loaded. Of course, I always thought I was fine. But she said I'd become verbally abusive to her and that she didn't want her kids growing up around that. When it became clear to her that I wasn't going to stop, not even after the doctor warned me, she just gave up on me.

"I felt terrible, of course. I didn't have any idea I was treating her like that. My own dad had been that way with my mother, and I hated it that I'd grown up to be just like him. I told her I was glad she left, that if she hadn't I would have ended up treating her a lot worse.

"We really talk now, more than we ever did before. I tell her about the things I'm worried about instead of keeping it all inside. They encourage us to do that at AA. I can honestly say we have a really good marriage now, something most musicians I know can't say.

"Being a musician is a perfect setup for becoming a drug abuser and alcoholic. There's so much intensity when you play publicly. You get high off the energy of the audience and the applause. Then the show is over and there is a gigantic letdown. You're away from home and all the other guys are using.

"But the best part about it all is how I feel every day. I feel *good.* I didn't know how bad I felt before. I mean, that stuff was killing me and I didn't even know it. Now my body isn't numb all the time and I have so much energy. My playing is better because I bring so much more to it. And my mind is clear. God, I can't believe what a difference that makes. I always thought I was playing really well but I wasn't. How could I be? I was loaded all the time. I really love playing now. I really get passionate about it. God, it's good to be alive."

Jennifer

Jennifer, like Micky, had to suffer a severe physical crisis before waking up to her problems.

"My heart attack was my wake-up call. I believe it was God's way of warning me that if I continued binging and purging I was going to die. I was in so much denial about having a problem that I don't think anyone or anything else could have convinced me to get help. But the heart attack really scared me into seeing the truth."

When Jennifer left the hospital she was immediately transferred to an eating disorders treatment clinic, where she stayed for two months.

"I was so humiliated when they transferred me to the center. I still didn't believe I belonged there with all those emaciated girls. It took me a long time to finally admit I had a problem and that I needed help as badly as I did. I always prided myself on being strong and in control. To admit I could also be weak and out of control when it came to food was extremely difficult for me.

"But looking back on it now, it was the best thing that ever happened to me. I began to explore the underlying causes of my problem and was educated about how women in this society are pressured into being thin. Gradually, I am beginning to accept my body just the way it is instead of trying to meet some media image of what is desirable."

While I do not believe God punishes us, I do believe God puts roadblocks in our way sometimes to get our attention, to teach us a lesson. An illness can be a reminder to honor our body. The loss of a business can be an indication that we need to get our priorities straight. Getting in trouble with the law can be a reminder that we have strayed too far from our own morals and values. A fall from grace can be a loving reminder that our life is out of balance.

13 An Invitation to Review Your Life

The unexamined life is
not worth living.

SOCRATES

You need only claim
the events of your life to make
yourself yours.

FLORIDA SCOTT-MAXWELL

One of the greatest blessings of a fall is that it can often cause us to review and reevaluate our life. People who fall from grace may experience the events of their lives flashing before their eyes, much like a near-death experience. Many people undergo transformations in their lives because of this. In this chapter I will give examples of those who, because of their fall, experienced a life review that changed their lives. I will also offer suggestions on how you can go about conducting your own life review.

Dannion Brinkley, in his book *Saved by the Light,* recalled the following details of his near-death experience:

> The Being of Light engulfed me, and as it did I began to experience my whole life, feeling and seeing everything that had ever happened to me. It was as though a dam had burst and every memory stored in my brain flowed out.
>
> The life review was not pleasant. From the moment it began until it ended, I was faced with the sickening reality that I had been an unpleasant person, someone who was self-centered and mean. [1]

Starting with what Dannion called his "angry childhood," he was forced to witness each and every negative, cruel or selfish act he had ever committed against another person. He saw himself mercilessly teasing other children, hitting teachers, stealing bicycles.

Each time he relived an incident he experienced the pain of those he had hurt. When he remembered a fist-fight he felt the anguish and humiliation his opponent

---

[1] Dannion Brinkley, *Saved by the Light* (New York: Villard Books, 1994), 10.

had felt. He also felt the grief he had caused his parents with his delinquent behavior.

"As my body lay dead on that stretcher, I was reliving every moment of my life, including my emotions, attitudes and motivations."[2]

Not only could he actually experience the way both he and the other person had felt when an incident took place, but he could also feel the emotions of the next individual to whom that person, in turn, reacted. "I was in a chain reaction of emotion, one that showed how deeply we affect one another."[3]

Like Dannion, many others who have had this type of near-death experience reported it to be a life-transforming experience. But you do not have to have a near-death experience to have such a transformation. You can experience this kind of transformation in this life, this realm.

In the following case, Adam describes how he saw his life flash before his eyes.

Adam

Adam, the surgeon who was passed over for chief of surgery and accused of sexual harassment, experienced his own form of life review several months after entering therapy with me.

"I had no idea people felt as they did about me," said Adam. "My wife . . . the people at work . . . God, what a shock! I mean, how can anyone be so blind? I was so wrapped up in myself and in my work that I simply didn't

[2] Brinkley, 14.
[3] Ibid., 14.

bother to pay attention to other people, not even my wife. As long as things went smoothly, I just kept on going, day after day. But this whole mess—the sexual harassment case, my wife almost leaving me—has opened my eyes. I've begun to remember things: all the times I forgot to buy my wife a present for our anniversary; the way she would look at me when I'd come home late for dinner; the times I missed my kids' birthday parties. And I remembered things about work, too. The time they all got together to throw me a surprise birthday party. I acted like such an asshole, like I was too busy to waste my time on a stupid party. Those people really went out of their way— they bought balloons and a cake, and a really nice present. But I didn't appreciate it and they could tell. They never threw me another party after that.

"And then this sexual harassment thing. God, I can't even believe it! When they first told me about it, I thought they were accusing me of pressuring these women for sex, and I was furious because I'd done no such thing. But when I got the official complaint from the Equal Employment Opportunity Commission [EEOC], I read that they weren't accusing me of that at all. They said it was my attitude. That I disrespected women and made inappropriate comments.

"As I read the papers, each and every one of the incidents came back to me. But this time I saw the situation from the woman's perspective. I hadn't meant it the way they took it, but I began to understand how they would feel. Like my comment to the one woman. She'd lost a lot of weight and I complimented her about it, told her she looked really great now. Really sexy. That she wasn't going to have a hard time catching a man now. I can see how she could have taken that as an insult. I was essentially saying she'd been unattractive before and that no man would have wanted her when she was overweight.

"And patting them on the behind. . . . The women said they didn't take it as me coming on to them but as a chauvinistic, patronizing kind of thing. They're absolutely right. I can't believe I did it."

Adam's newfound awareness about the effect he had on other people was just the beginning of some profound changes in his life. In the following months we reviewed his life for the causes of his behavior.

"Being a surgeon is a very heady experience. People's lives are in your hands. If you aren't careful, you can begin to feel like God. That's essentially what happened to me. I got to the place where I felt so powerful I didn't feel like I needed to think about other people's feelings. And I felt my work was more important than anything else: my marriage, my kids, my work relationships. Now I realize that all these things are equally important."

My Fall

I now realize that the purpose of my fall was to get me to review my life, take a close look at how I had treated others, and face some important things about myself. Although less dramatic than Dannion Brinkley's near-death experience, mine was equally sobering. I, too, came to vividly remember all the damage I had done to others and to experience their pain, disappointment and anger.

I remembered all the people who had been kind to me but whom, in my arrogant, narcissistic fashion, I had taken for granted, been insensitive to or, in some instances, been cruel toward. I recalled from a totally different perspective my past love relationships and realized that while I had always seen myself as a victim, in most cases I was not. In fact, in some cases I was even the abuser. There had been people who had truly loved me and I had returned their love with jealousy, possessiveness and endless demands.

Like Dannion Brinkley, I learned that love is the most important expression in life and that I had been too busy demanding it from others to give it. While I gave understanding and compassion to my clients, I did not give the same to my loved ones, most especially to my own mother.

The following exercise will help you conduct your own life review, to take stock of your life, and accept responsibility for the hurt and pain you have caused others.

1. Make a list of all the people you remember hurting in your life.
2. Now put yourself in every person's place. Imagine how they must have felt. Try to experience their pain, humiliation and anger.
3. Think about what you learned from this experience.
4. Write about how this experience has changed you.

You may discover that empathy does not come easily to you. If this is the case, you may have to teach yourself to have empathy for others by practicing putting yourself in their place, in order to feel their emotions and experience what they must have experienced.

In addition to gaining an awareness of their cruel or heartless behavior and the effect it has had on others, some people, through a life review, gained insight about other aspects of themselves that they had never faced before. This was the case with former model Melody, whom you met earlier.

Melody

"My fall from grace made me finally take stock of my life, and I didn't like what I saw," said Melody. "From the time I was a little girl, my life was centered around how I looked. That's how I got attention and admiration, especially from men. I grew up believing that the only thing that made me special was my beauty. So when my looks started to go, I began to panic.

"I finally came to realize that modeling was just an extension of my need to be admired. The only reason I wanted to model or act was because I wanted to be adored by thousands of people. I wanted to see myself in magazines, on television, even on the big screen, and imagine all the people watching me, wanting me. When that didn't pan out, I found that being adored by rich and famous men was a good substitute.

"Then when I stopped getting the attention I was used to from men, I didn't know what to do. I was finally faced with the real possibility that I might end up all alone.

"When Joe offered me that acting job, I thought of it as my last chance. I knew I was too old to be hired for my beauty anymore, and I wasn't sure of my talent. So it's interesting that I blew it with Joe by having that affair with Chad. I knew Joe still had a thing for me.

"I realize now that I sabotaged the role because I knew I couldn't act. I was afraid I was going to make a fool of myself in front of all those people. So instead, I made Joe mad so he'd fire me. Of course, all this was on a subconscious level. And I hadn't expected him to humiliate me in front of all those people.

"I was forced to look inside myself, and what I found was emptiness. My entire life had been focused on beauty—my own looks, acquiring beautiful things, being surrounded by beautiful people and living in beautiful surroundings. It was almost an obsession.

"But the truth was, I felt ugly inside. I'd been a spoiled, egotistical child with the men I was with, always demanding attention, insisting on my own way. I didn't stop to think of other people's feelings, only my own.

"I became so depressed after all this that I almost killed myself one night when I was drunk and high on cocaine. That scared me enough to get me into therapy."

What Melody discovered in therapy was that she was enraged with men, most especially her father. He was, after all, the person who gave her the message that her self-worth was dependent on her looks. He focused so much on how beautiful she was, and how much he loved her for her beauty, that she grew to believe he wouldn't love her if she *weren't* beautiful. And he spoiled her so much and provided so few rules that she grew up with a feeling of *entitlement*—a belief that she *deserved* special treatment. She also learned early on that she could manipulate people to get what she wanted. All this no doubt contributed to the narcissistic personality disorder she suffered from, which, in turn, prevented her from developing meaning and depth to her life.

There are several ways of conducting a life review. Psychotherapy can be a form of life review. Those who practice a 12-Step program also undergo a life review as they complete the steps. The following information and questions, taken from my forthcoming book, *Reviewing Your Life,* offers suggestions as to how you can continue your personal life-review process.

Discovering Your Life Lessons

Although we may look at our lives as a series of unrelated, seemingly meaningless events and coincidences, there is, in fact, a pattern and meaning to everyone's life. Most psychologists and spiritual leaders know this to be true. While they may interpret the patterns in a person's life differently, both groups share the belief that there is little likelihood that events occur in a person's life that are merely happenstance or coincidence. Psychologists refer to "the repetition compulsion" to explain the fact that people repeatedly make the same kinds of mistakes, or that they continue to get involved with the same kind of people over and over again. But even psychologists believe that the psychological reasons why we repeat patterns is only half the answer. There is another reason—a deeper, more spiritual reason—for what happens to us.

In the movie *Defending Your Life,* the protagonist, played by Albert Brooks, is killed in a car accident and is sent to a place called Judgment City, where he is shown episodes from nine days of his life. These episodes are significant moments in his life, all with something in common: They all show incidents when fear stopped him from acting. The purpose of showing him these events was to remind him of all the times in his life when he didn't face his fears. It was his job to convince the judges that he had learned his life lesson and should therefore be allowed to proceed to heaven instead of being sent back to earth for another lifetime. We learn that he has been sent back to earth five times before and get the picture that he is having a rather difficult time learning his life lesson.

Through the ages, religious leaders and philosophers have told us that each of us is put on earth for a purpose, and that each of us has lessons to learn. Some believe we must learn our lessons before we go on to the next level.

Many religions believe we take with us everything we are, every thought and every emotion, to our next life or level. They believe that we have a chance, up to the last minute of our life, to let go of some of the pain, anger and fear that has held us down in our lives, and that the more we release, the less we take into our next life.

Many believe that in order to continue evolving emotionally and spiritually, we must learn certain life lessons. It doesn't matter what your religious beliefs are; finding your life's lessons applies to all beliefs. Most religions believe there is a hereafter, a heaven, or someplace where life is better than it is on earth.

Today a growing number of people believe that they have lessons to learn in life, but usually need some direction to discover what they are.

In the movie, the protagonist had his life lessons spelled out for him. Except for those who are fortunate enough to have this done for them by a trusted spiritual leader or guide, or for those who have had a near-death experience where they were shown their entire lives, most of us are not this fortunate. Many of us live our

entire lives trying to figure out just what we are supposed to be learning, sensing that there is more to life
than meets the eye, but never really knowing what.
Most people have had to discover their life lessons the
hard way, through crisis, illness and trauma. Most learn
their life lessons just before death, when everything
seems to fall into place and they see their lives flash
before their eyes. But we don't have to wait for impend-
ing death because there is another way to have this life-
transforming experience.

Biographers look back on someone's life and see the
patterns, the pivotal moments, the crucial decisions
that created the events of a person's life. How sad that
most people do not take the time to review their own
life the way a biographer would—dispassionately and
objectively. The following exercises and series of questions can help you to do this.

Your Life Story

Find a place where you will not be disturbed. I recommend lying down in a darkened room, but you may
also choose to sit up. Put paper and a pen where you can
easily reach them. Please read the following instructions
completely before beginning. When they are clear in
your mind, begin the exercise.

1. Take some deep breaths and clear your mind of all
   thoughts. Think of your life as if it were a movie.
   Imagine that you have a magic button you can push
   that will rewind your life, much like you can do

with a video recorder. Keep going back until you have reached your very first memory. Now go forward and remember another significant scene from your life. Continue playing your movie (your life) in your mind, picking out the most significant scenes.

2. Open your eyes and go back over your memories. Choose moments in time when you experienced an intense emotion; moments when time stood still; moments that stand out from all the rest and those that have been etched in your memory. Write these memories down.

Don't write just the major events of your life. When you choose a scene, there should be a significant emotional charge to it. In fact, major events might not make it to your list at all. Don't take too much time thinking; just write as events come to your mind. Let your life flash before you. Breathe deeply. You might be surprised by the events you have chosen and the ones you have skipped over.

3. Now go over your list and put a star or two stars beside those that really stand out: all those that still get to you, make your stomach flip-flop, bring back intense feelings or hold an emotional charge. Try to narrow your list to less than 10 items. If you can't seem to do this, put the list aside for a while and come back to it later. Your attachment to certain items may change when you take a fresh look at the list. You'll need to eliminate some memorable experiences and this can be difficult, but try not to let your ego or any preconceived ideas get in the way.

4. Working with just the starred items, write about the incidents and why they were so significant, powerful and meaningful to you.

5. Using what you have written, condense or characterize the experiences to only a few words. Examples: loneliness, fear, hope, friendship.

6. Now circle the key words in your condensed version—again, select only those words that really stand out.

This experience can be an important beginning for your life review, and can provide you with some key words to work with. These words have meaning only for you, and you may use them as you wish. They may hold the key to deeper insights, represent clues to your life lessons, or support issues you are already working on.

Lessons from Your Family Legacy

Every family has certain patterns of behavior that are shared among family members and passed down from generation to generation. The following questions can help you to uncover these patterns.

1. Where were you born? Where were each of your parents, grandparents, great-grandparents born? (Research as far back as you can.) What messages did you receive about your national origin and the origin of your family?

2. Which religion were you raised to follow? Were you raised to believe that your religion was the

only true one? What were the main messages you remember receiving from your religion about yourself and life in general?

3. Was your family or anyone in your family the object of prejudice? Would you characterize your family as being prejudiced against any group of people?

4. What were some of the stories about your family that were passed down from generation to generation?

5. Characterize your family. Going back as many generations as you are able, how would you describe it?

6. How would you describe your immediate family of origin (your parents, siblings, yourself)?

7. Is there a history of alcoholism or heavy drinking in your family? What about drugs, prescription or otherwise?

8. Is there a history of mental illness or bizarre behavior in your family?

9. Is there a history of criminal behavior in your family? Was anyone in your family ever a victim of a crime? What messages did you receive about obeying the law?

10. Is there a history of sexual addiction or sexual abuse in your family? Was anyone in your family a victim of child sexual abuse or rape? What messages did you receive about sex?

11. What was the economic status of: your immediate family of origin; your grandparents; great-grandparents, etc.? What messages did you receive about the importance of money?

12. How did your family members resolve conflicts among themselves? Did they argue, talk things over rationally or ignore conflicts entirely? Do the people in your family get along? Is there a history of family members not talking to one another for long periods of time? Do you get along with members of your family today?

13. How does your family view divorce? Is there a history of divorce in your family? What were the reasons for divorce?

14. Has there been much illness in your family? If so, describe the illnesses. What was the message you received from these illnesses?

15. Do people in your family tend to live a long time or die early? What is the average age at death? Have there been any accidental deaths (including war) or murders in your family?

From what you have discovered so far, what messages would you say make up your family legacy? Examples: "Our family is superior to other families," "Life is painful," "Money is the answer to most problems," "There is something wrong with my family and with me," "The Irish are lazy drunks but we have a great sense of humor and tend to be talented."

The following suggestions will help you to transform the anger and negativity surrounding your family legacy into life lessons.

- Let yourself feel. Really think about yourself as the culmination, the embodiment of all the good and bad traits that have been passed down to you from both sides of your family. Feel the wholeness of that—the richness of it. You wouldn't be who you are today if you didn't embody all the characteristics of both your mother's and your father's sides of the family.

- Notice your body and the traits (good and bad) that you've inherited from both sides of your family. You wouldn't be who you are without these physical traits.
- Think about the most negative characteristic or problem that you've inherited (alcoholism, bigotry, criticalness). Notice what lessons you've learned from having that problem. What have you learned from having to work on this problem? Example: empathy for others with similar problems.
- Think about a positive trait that you inherited from your family. Notice the good things you have done in your life because of this trait. Notice the good that has come back to you.
- Why do you think you chose to be born into this particular family? What life lessons were you to learn from being in this family?
- Write a fable or fairy tale about your family or about the life of, and lessons learned by, one significant person in your family.

My Life Review

My own search for my family legacy was very poignant. I uncovered a history of narcissism, alcoholism, bigotry and emotional abuse. But I also learned that I inherited tremendous creativity, intelligence and a sense of humor.

I realized that the traits I hated most in my mother and in other members of my family were those I also possessed. I had always perceived myself as being very different from them, and yet I was strikingly similar. I buried these traits under my public persona of being magnanimous, nonjudgmental and caring, but they were just underneath the surface.

My greatest teacher has turned out to be the unlikeliest person. It is someone who plagued my life from birth, someone I had always blamed for ruining my life and making it a "holy hell," someone I swore didn't know how to love, a person who was one of the most judgmental people I'd ever known. This person was my mother—my nemesis, my enemy, my abuser.

How did this unlikely turn of events transpire? During a time when my mother and I were no longer speaking to one another, she read and was transformed by my book, *The Emotionally Abused Woman*. Ironically, I had also been transformed while writing it, and so when she called to say "I'm sorry," the words I had longed to hear from her for years, I was in a very nonjudgmental state of mind. I accepted her apology and we slowly began to heal the rift that had been between us for years.

I then saw my mother as a product of the same criticism, neglect, narcissism and alcoholism that I was. She had treated me as she had been treated. I no longer judged her or myself.

I truly believe it was all a part of my life plan to experience my fall from grace, to write and learn from my book, *The Emotionally Abused Woman,* and then to pass on the information to my mother.

Messages from Your Body

This series of questions can be particularly powerful for those who feel their fall was caused by an imbalance of the body, or whose fall involved sickness or an accident that caused physical damage.

1. What messages were you given (by parents, parental example and family background) about caring for your body?
2. How much importance did your parents and other family members place on physical appearance?
3. Did you get the impression that your parents liked or disliked, approved or disapproved of your physical appearance?
4. Whom do you most resemble in your family? What feedback did you receive from other family members concerning this resemblance?
5. Do you believe you were treated poorly because of your likeness to another family member (i.e., because you reminded your mother of your father, who deserted her)?
6. Did any of your physical features cause you embarrassment as a child?
7. What names were you called because of your physical appearance as a child?
8. What major physical illnesses have you suffered in your life? How did these illnesses affect you?
9. What surgeries have you had in your life? How did these surgeries affect you?

10. What physical handicaps do you have? How have those handicaps affected you?

11. What part of your body do you like the least?

12. What part of your body do you like the most?

13. What part of your body would you change if you could? How do you imagine the change would affect your life?

14. Make a list of all the messages you remember receiving about your body from the time you were a child until the present. Include verbal and non-verbal messages from your parents, nicknames and insults from your siblings and peers, and criticism from friends and lovers. Put a star beside each message that still has an effect on you (those you still believe, those that are still replayed in your head).

15. Make a list of all the messages you received about your sexual organs, masturbation and your sexual attractiveness. Put a star beside each message that still has an impact on you.

16. List the ways your body has been misused, mistreated or abused by other people.

17. List the ways in which you mistreat or abuse your body. Why do you believe you do these things?

18. How do you show respect, love and caring for your body today?

19. What is your biggest concern about your body today?

20. What lesson concerning your body do you believe you are now working on?

My hope is that these questions and exercises will be helpful to you in your life-review process. There are many other areas of your life to question, including traumas and crises, career and avocation, personal relationships, your dark side. As you continue reviewing your life, you will discover some of your life lessons. The following information may also help you with this discovery.

Most people discover that their life lesson is a version of one of the following:

1. To learn to be less judgmental/critical
2. To learn to be forgiving
3. To learn and practice gratitude
4. To learn to be less envious of others
5. To learn patience, that everything is as it should be
6. To learn that we are all both good *and* bad
7. To learn that we create what we fear

When you have completed your life review, in whatever form it takes, another phase of spiritual healing will begin to occur. Recognizing that you now have the rest of your life ahead of you to change will give you real hope. Dannion Brinkley described the experience this way:

> I had felt the pain and anguish of reflection, but from that I had gained the knowledge that I could use to correct my life. I could hear the Being's message in my head, again as if through telepathy: "Humans are powerful spiritual beings meant to create good on the earth. This good isn't usually accomplished in bold actions, but in singular acts of kindness between people. It's the little things

that count, because they are more spontaneous and show who you truly are." [4]

If we don't learn our lessons in life, events will repeat themselves to force us to address them. Sometimes we aren't aware of our life lessons until we experience a crisis, an illness or a significant separation. And then, in the midst of crises, many of us finally realize that life is trying to tell us something. We can either get the message now or have it repeated, in the form of another crisis, another wake-up call.

Basic Concepts of the Life Review

- There are lessons to be learned from everything we do and from everything that happens to us.
- We each have the ability to decipher and understand these lessons.
- Life presents us with one experience after another until we learn a particular lesson.
- If we don't learn a particular lesson, it will be presented to us again and again.
- When we learn the lesson, the cycle stops.
- We may not always get what we want, but we get what we need.

---

[4] Brinkley, 20-21.

An Opportunity to Complete Unfinished Business, Connect and Heal Your True Self

I had to walk through the past
so I could have a future.

MICHELE PILLAR CARLTON

Closely related to an invitation to review your life is the blessing that comes with an opportunity to complete unfinished business from the past. While reviewing your life tends to help you get a better picture of your entire life—where you are going, and what lessons you need to learn—completing unfinished business helps you to clear up the debris from the past that is getting in the way of your future.

Richard Berendzen

In *Come Here,* Richard Berendzen writes: "I believed in the power of my own will. Self-determination I learned about later by reading about leaders I admired. Man is the master of his fate. Whenever the abuse came into my mind, I would say, 'I'm not going to think about this.' It was my way to fight back. I couldn't stop the abuse, but I could, through force of will, stop myself from thinking about it. Denial became synonymous with survival. How could it hurt me if I didn't think about it?" [1]

But Richard's past *was* hurting him, and signs of it began seeping through the cracks. After his father's death, he started making phone calls to strangers who had placed ads in newspapers to provide child care. He'd chat briefly with these people and then insinuate something about children and sexuality. For example, he would mention that in his home his children bathed with his wife and himself, or that they slept in the same bed. Usually the other people expressed no interest or would say they didn't do such things in their home. Most calls were no longer than 10 minutes, and then he'd quickly end the conversation.

This continued for several years, but in 1990 he began to suffer from feelings of depression and to make the calls more frequently. One day, he called the wrong woman (or as it turned out, the *right* woman). This woman didn't end the conversation when he hinted at parents and children being sexually involved. Instead, she spoke to him at length and encouraged him to call again. When he did call her back, he made up stories about bizarre sexual activities that he and his wife did with their children.

---

[1] Berendzen, 24.

Unbeknownst to him, the police had attached a device to her phone to record and trace his calls.

"As much as I found the calls repulsive, the compulsion to call again grew even stronger," Richard confessed. "Part of my life had spun out of control. I was too ashamed and baffled to tell anyone about it. How would I begin? Ninety-nine percent of me was the man the world saw: university president, husband, father. But the other one percent was a bomb about to explode and destroy everything I stood for and had worked to achieve." [2]

Sometimes a crisis such as a fall will cause repressed and suppressed memories to surface, as they did in Richard's case.

"I now know I lived two childhoods, the one I remembered and the one I repressed. The one I remembered was the one that made it possible for me to survive. I was 51 years old before I remembered some of the repressed parts. [3]

"As a young boy, I found that if I worked hard, I could forget about my feelings. The switch that gave me mastery over my situation was denial. If I didn't think about the trauma, I could forget it—perhaps forever. And if I forgot it, it effectively hadn't happened." [4]

Many people never consider seeking psychotherapy or even confiding in another person about troubling issues from their past until prompted by their fall from grace. Richard explained it this way:

"I had never really confided in anyone except my wife, and clearly, before Hopkins I had never told her the real

[2] Berendzen, 7.
[3] Ibid., 24.
[4] Ibid., 85.

story about myself. I would not have gone down like a kamikaze pilot in my own life if I had started talking years before.

"The sad thing is that no one could have convinced me to start talking. I had no idea—and could not have been persuaded—that something from so long ago suddenly could take over my life. I want others to know what I learned—if you have been traumatized by abuse, you must find a way to understand and resolve it. Even if your life seems fine at the moment, unresolved trauma neither goes away nor diminishes over time. It can erupt at any time." [5]

An eruption of this sort is often the cause of a fall from grace.

Connecting with and Healing Our True Selves

A fall from grace also affords us the unique opportunity to connect with and heal our true selves. What is our "self"? As Marsha Sinetar writes in her wonderful book, *Elegant Choices, Healing Choices:*

> Our "self" is not something we find in the determinations, judgments or descriptions of another. Our self is an essential being—inside us, inside our skins, a core being, to be experienced, nurtured, known and loved (even created—in a way—outwardly) so that self can vigorously express itself in the world. [6]

[5] Berendzen, 251.
[6] Marsha Sinetar, *Elegant Choices, Healing Choices: Finding Grace and Wholeness in Everything We Choose* (New York: Paulist Press, 1988), 45.

Some people differentiate between our self and our *true* self. Our true self is usually described as the truest and best of us, the self that we are in our best moments. Lewis Smedes describes it this way:

> Our true self is like a design for a building still under construction or the original design for a building that needs restoring. It is stamped in the depths of us like a template for the selves we are meant to be and yet are failing to be.
>
> Christians recognize the pattern of their true selves in the story of Jesus. We may also recognize it when we see it in the lives of our heroes and saints. We feel it in the pressure we get from our own conscience when it works right. We know it by a deep intuition we have of the better person we would be if we truly were all we could be. [7]

The false self, on the other hand, is our image of what we *think* we should be based on false ideals imposed on us by other people. These false ideals are planted in us by three sources: (1) our parents, (2) the culture in which we live and (3) religion.

Many people believe that sin is the split, or separation, from self. The separation from self is what causes us to act against our best interests, to make errors in judgment and to betray ourselves. When we are disconnected from self we become controlled by fear, self-doubt and self-criticism. We cannot be counted on to think or act correctly.

---

[7] Smedes, 32-33.

How do we get in touch with our true self? First and foremost, it is through our emotions. Paying attention to and honoring your feelings will help you get past the layers of your public self, your "all-good self," to the real person you are at your core.

And how do we heal our true self? Marsha Sinetar believes that:

> Beauty heals. Truth heals. Coherence and order heal. Courage, valor, honor—all of these qualities heal us. And by "heal" I mean *make whole*, patch up any split in ourselves that still exists. When we are strongly centered and connected to Self, our spontaneous choices are more likely to be true, courageous and attractive. [8]

Max

Max, the movie director who experienced a tremendous fall when his work suddenly went out of vogue, was forced for the first time in his life to discover his self.

When Max first came to see me he was desperate for help. He said he had hit bottom in his life. He talked about feelings of emptiness inside, of having no motivation and little will to live. He also told me he had realized that he didn't know who he was anymore, or rather, that he'd *never* known who he was.

"I don't care how much time it takes or how painful it is, I want to discover me," Max told me. "I can't go on this way—being this depressed, just existing. And now I don't

---

[8] Sinetar, 19.

know if I want to go back to the way things were, even if I could. There's got to be more to life than making movies and bedding women. Somehow, I've gone past that. But I don't have any idea what else there is for me."

I was happy Max had hit bottom because in my experience, this is usually the only time someone with strong narcissistic tendencies like Max had will ever seek help. Max's depression was not only what brought him into therapy, but also a sign that his healing had begun. And I was glad that he had the motivation to work at finding out who he was because it was going to be a painful process.

We worked on helping him to recognize and identify his true emotions and to begin to find the real Max underneath all the layers of facade. It was indeed a painful process and several times he threatened to quit. With the help of more than two years of intensive therapy, Max is now beginning to discover who he is at his core. The last time I saw him he told me, "Now I don't have to continually reinvent myself—I can just be."

There is another aspect of our self that we often lose touch with, and that is our body. Adrienne, whom you were introduced to in chapter 7, discovered that her bout with chronic fatigue syndrome was the catalyst that forced her to connect with and heal her relationship with her body.

Adrienne

"Before I got sick, I was so out of touch with my body I wasn't even aware of it most of the time," Adrienne confided. "I was always in my head—you know—always

thinking, analyzing, fantasizing. My body was just something I needed to carry my head around.

"It wasn't until I started getting sick that I began to
appreciate and connect with my body. It's ironic. People
like Christopher Reeve talk about how we are so much
more than our bodies and we *are*. But for me it was
important to reconnect with my body and to appreciate
all it provides.

"When I was sick I was so angry with my body. I felt
like it was the cause of all my problems. It had made me
lose my boyfriend, my job, my friends, my self-respect. It
had even made me question my sanity.

"Since then, I've begun to make friends with my body,
to really get to know it. That may sound funny, but I really
do believe that the reason I got sick was because I was so
disconnected from my body. Now I'm much more in tune
with my body and its needs."

Like Adrienne, many of us have spent years being
emotionally disconnected from our bodies. This
estrangement is inevitable, considering that we have
been taught to regard the mind as separate from the
body, and to think of ourselves not as bodies but as
intellects who own, or have, bodies.

The extent to which we experience this alienation is
made most apparent when we are ill or when our
body does not perform the way we want it to. Instead
of seeing our body and mind in partnership, we see
our body as the enemy—as betraying us or spoiling
our good times, or as getting in the way of our career,
our relationship or whatever else has been disrupted
by the illness.

The following exercises have proved to be excellent methods for helping people to connect with their bodies and create a more positive body image.

The Mirror Exercise

Set up a full-length mirror in a place where you can have privacy. Undress in front of the mirror, noticing whether the room is sufficiently warm enough for you to be comfortable in the nude. Now begin to carefully examine your body with a neutral, curious eye—not a critical one. It might help to maintain a neutral attitude if you talk out loud, describing what you see, starting from your head and going all the way down to your toes. For example: "My hair is brown and curly. My forehead is high. My eyes are hazel and attractive. My lips are full and sensual. . . ."

If you find that looking at yourself naked is a bit frightening and uncomfortable, you're not alone. Most people, especially women, find it difficult to look at their naked bodies. If you find this is true for you, keep trying, even if it means discontinuing the exercise and trying again at another time.

Look at your body from all angles and in various positions—sitting, bending over, kneeling. Use a hand mirror or a second full-length mirror to see your back. Continue to look at yourself for at least 15 minutes, even though you may feel embarrassed and inhibited.

Once you have some idea of how you look, work on letting go of your need to chastise yourself for your real or imagined imperfections. Try looking at yourself in an objective, nonjudgmental way—perhaps the way you might look at a friend. Say aloud to your reflection in the mirror, "You're okay. Your body's fine. I like what I see."

Repeat this exercise a few days later. If you are like most people, you may need to complete the exercise at least two to three times before you notice any change in your attitude toward your body. Once you are able to look at yourself naked in the mirror without criticism or disappointment, you will gradually begin to feel a sense of familiarity and acceptance.

The Self-Love Exercise

As you look at each part of your body, verbally express love to it just as you would to the body of a beloved child. Thank your body for all that it does for you. Think of all the ways each part of your body helps you and all the ways each part brings pleasure into your life. For example, thank your feet for carrying you around, for helping you walk and run and dance, for providing balance. Thank your stomach for storing and processing your food, for protecting your inner organs. Thank your spine for holding up your frame and for allowing you to bend over.

A fall from grace can be an opportunity for you to clear up unresolved issues from the past and to reconnect with your true self. Take this opportunity, relish it, and allow it to provide you with a new beginning.

15

A Test or Renewal of Your Faith

Like steel that has been
passed through fire . . . stronger
for having been tested.

ELIZABETH DUNCAN KOONTZ

It is by surmounting difficulties, not
by sinking under them, that
we discover our fortitude.

HANNAH WEBSTER FORTES

Some people are concerned that a crisis or fall from grace will cause them to lose faith in their creator. But often, a fall causes us to regain or renew our belief in our creator and to reach out in desperation and humility to a power greater than our own. When we are in crisis, we are more inclined to look outside ourselves for help, and in so doing put aside our arrogant belief that we are totally in control of our lives.

There is a higher power who is *really* in charge. And a fall from grace is sometimes a painful reminder of this. It may take a tragedy, a painful failure, the humiliation and shame of a fall to humble us enough to bring us to our knees.

It may have taken a fall from grace for you to finally give up trying to control things, for you to raise your head to the heavens and cry out, "Please, dear God, please help me." It is in that moment of complete surrender that everything changes. When we surrender our will, surrender our belief that we are totally in control, we are met with overwhelming peace and grace. This is often the most meaningful lesson and the most wonderful blessing we can receive from our fall.

During my fall and several times since, I have experienced the tremendous relief and subsequent peace that comes from finally saying to God, "I give up. Please help me. Please." For some reason I have to get to a place of utter hopelessness before I finally surrender, and yet each time I do, I am reminded of how healing it is and how much it changes everything.

When we finally pray for and believe in the words

"Thy will be done," our life changes. All it takes is for us to let go and place our problem in higher hands. You will never know the liberation this prayer can bring until you say it.

Richard Berendzen described his experience of finally letting go and placing his life in God's hands:

> "Thy will be done," not mine. I don't know where the words came from. I had known the Lord's Prayer since childhood, but it wasn't in my mind. Although I don't know why those words came to me then, I do know what happened next. I felt a rush of tranquility. Having relinquished control, I felt more centered and stable than I had since the crisis began, or perhaps since my life began. Releasing control differed from giving up; I didn't give up, I let go. Okay, here I am. Show me what to do. It's your move.[1]

Those of us who tend to be arrogant and controlling may not be able to learn this lesson any other way but to experience a fall from grace. We are too convinced that we alone are in charge of our lives, that we need no one, that we are invincible. While being self-actualized (knowing what you want and believing that by your will and drive you can attain it) is a wonderful quality, one that many people do not have, we also need to be reminded to exercise our humility and gratitude toward our creator, the source of all our strengths and gifts. Whether you believe that your

---

[1] Berendzen, 164-165.

creator is God, the universe, Great Spirit, the
Goddesses—it makes no difference. The point is that
we are not the sole creator of our own destiny.
Someone or something is guiding us, making it possible for us to live on this earth and benefit from all
the riches of this planet.

Even those who are devoutly religious may have their
faith renewed as a result of their fall from grace, as you
will learn from Michele's experience.

Michele Pillar Carlton

"I learned a valuable lesson from my fall, a lesson I
wish to pass on to other Christians who may be struggling
as I did. No one told me when I first became a Christian
that while salvation is instantaneous, it takes a lifetime to
become Christ-like. You need time to heal from abuse and
neglect, even if you are a Christian. I believe there are a
whole lot of people walking around feeling badly about
themselves because they aren't as Christ-like as they
would like to be. If you're still fighting with a monster
after all these years, it's okay. It doesn't mean you aren't a
good Christian. You don't have to be perfect in God's eyes.
God's love is unconditional, not based on performance.
He's already taken care of your sins, already forgiven you.
He isn't shocked by your actions, no matter what they are.

"I feel so grateful that I didn't lose my faith like so many
others have. God preserved my ability to minister to
people and I believe my fall from grace has helped me to
do just that."

God truly does speak to us in mysterious ways.

16 Blessings in Abundance

Dost thou wish to receive mercy?
Show mercy to thy neighbor.

St. John Chrysostom

The secret of contentment is the
realization that life is a
gift, not a right.

Anonymous

I n addition to those I've mentioned, there are many, many more blessings that may be bestowed on us after a fall. From our trials we may learn to become more compassionate and empathetic toward others, less critical and judgmental, and more grateful and humble.

Learning to Be Less Judgmental and More Compassionate

We tend to be judgmental and critical of others because we lack empathy for their position. When we judge other people we, in essence, put ourselves in a position *above* them. When we have empathy, however, we put ourselves in *their place.* Judging is a position of *superiority.* Empathy is a position of *equality.*

Having empathy for others is the ability to put oneself in their place and to imagine how they must feel at any given time. Compassion, on the other hand, is not only having a sympathetic consciousness of another's distress but also the desire to alleviate it. Sometimes it takes a fall to teach us both.

We can add many benefits to our daily life when we move from judgment to empathy. For example, judging others keeps us separate from other people and prevents us from being as loving as we can be to those we care about. It also prevents us from dealing with our own issues. It is easier to judge others than to remind ourselves that we, too, are fallible, vulnerable human beings with rage, fear, greed and envy in our hearts. In addition, if we don't stop judging others, we will continue to experience the judgment of others.

Father Murphy

"The greatest blessing from my fall was that I learned to be more compassionate and empathetic toward others," Father Murphy confessed. "Before my fall I was a pompous, judgmental man. I felt *above* those who sinned, as if my being a priest made me immune to sin. I'd tell myself, 'I could never do such a thing.'

"When I first began to have sexual fantasies and feelings about being with a child sexually, I was mortified. I prayed to God to take such vile thoughts away from me, to cleanse me of such perversity. I had always seen myself as such a pious man, a man who was above such depravity. But suddenly I had been cast down among all the other sinners. This changed my attitude about those who had sinned. I no longer felt as judgmental of others.

"It's ironic, I know, that a priest should feel judgmental, since we believe so strongly in forgiveness and in the power of confession. But be that as it may, I was extremely judgmental and arrogant. Being a priest can do that to you. You begin believing that because you live such an exemplary life you are better than others. And because others revere you so, it is difficult *not* to view yourself as being above them.

"I damaged that boy in ways that he will never get over, and I will always feel terrible for what I did to him. I no longer feel I have the right to judge anyone. It became painfully clear to me that we are *all* the same, so-called saints and sinners. We *all* have a dark side, we are *all* fallen angels."

There is, indeed, a real danger in believing we are above others. We lose our compassion, and become pompous and narrow-minded.

The following exercise will help you to be less judgmental of others.

1. Recall a recent argument or disagreement you had with someone.
2. Focus on remembering any judgmental, pompous attitudes you may have had during the exchange.
3. Attempt to view the exchange from the other person's point of view.
4. View the exchange again, this time with the new information in mind. Do you see the exchange differently?

An important aspect of learning to be less judgmental is to own our Shadow, or dark side. All of us are capable of committing selfish or cruel acts, a fact that most of us fail to accept. So-called negative emotions and behaviors—rage, jealousy, shame, resentment, lust, greed—lie concealed just beneath the surface, masked by our more proper selves. Those who know this about themselves and others will tend to be less judgmental. Those who will not or cannot admit to their own human frailties are the most judgmental of the frailties of others.

Sometimes we are aware of our Shadow, and out of fear of being propelled into acting in ways that we will regret, we consciously work at suppressing and controlling our more unacceptable urges. More often, though, we are entirely unaware of it. One of the many ways that we attempt to keep our Shadow at bay is by projecting it onto others in the form of judgments.

As you work on becoming less judgmental and more empathetic, it is important to remember these points.

- Your judgment of others often has more to do with you than with them.
- When we judge we take the focus off of ourselves.
- Be careful whom you judge—you may soon be in their shoes.
- When we judge we are likely to misjudge.
- When we judge we are putting ourselves above others.
- When we judge we are choosing to ignore the fact that perhaps:
    we have done the same thing;
    we have considered doing the same thing;
    we have come close to doing the same thing.

The following list explains who is most likely to have difficulty when attempting to experience the feeling of someone else's condition.

- Someone who is uncomfortable with her own emotions will probably not be particularly responsive to another's.
- Someone who is anxiously monitoring her own internal state or behavior will be similarly handicapped—i.e., "I cannot listen to my child with empathy if I am inwardly preoccupied with being a good mother."

- Someone who is more interested in analyzing the other than in imagining and resonating to that person's feelings will have difficulty empathizing with another person.
- Someone whose own needs seem more pressing than those of the other is also unlikely to attend fully to the other person.
- Someone who feels drained of energy by the demands of others is unlikely to feel sympathy for them.

Self-esteem is another factor in determining a person's ability to be empathetic toward others. In fact, there seems to be a direct relationship between self-esteem and the ability to be empathetic. I define self-esteem as a core of respect for and faith in oneself, an acceptance of one's own worth that is not contingent (at least not for an adult) on acceptance from others or on a certain level of accomplishment.

Those who feel good about themselves may be more inclined to empathize with others than those who are preoccupied with personal inadequacies and other concerns about the self. Conversely, a poor self-concept makes it more difficult to extend the boundaries of the self in benevolent ways. It seems that high self-esteem increases our responsiveness to others' needs by freeing us from the self-absorption that a precarious view of our worth can generate.

My Story

Like Father Murphy, I, too, learned to be less judgmental due to my fall. I had been extremely judgmental of my mother for being so narcissistic and emotionally abusive, as I had been of all my clients' parents who had been neglectful or abusive of them. But as I slowly faced my own narcissism and abusiveness, I found it harder and harder to judge others. I knew how hard it was for me to finally acknowledge my own problems, and for the first time I came to realize how very difficult it is for all of us to admit our problems, especially when we discover how much we may have damaged someone else. I learned just how humiliating it is to own up to negative behavior if you've always seen yourself as a victim or someone who really cared about people.

Many people grow up with inadequate or inappropriate training in how to be empathetic. But it is never too late to learn empathy. For example, think of someone you are having difficulties with and write about the situation from the perspective of that person. Or imagine how a loved one would describe you to another person, or imagine you are a fly on the wall while your mate, child or friend talks about your relationship.

Cultivating a Grateful Spirit

I move through my day-to-day life
with a sense of appreciation and gratitude that
comes from knowing how fortunate I truly am and

how unearned all that I am thankful for really is.
To have this perspective in my everyday
consciousness is in itself a gift, for it leads to
feeling "graced," or blessed, each time.

JEAN SHINODA BOLEN

Many people who have experienced a fall learned they needed to begin to practice gratitude. Those who experienced a financial fall had not appreciated what they had, were never satisfied and constantly wanted more. Those who lost a spouse may have taken the relationship for granted. Those who experienced a major illness or accident found that they weren't appreciating their body.

Regardless of our religious backgrounds, from the time we are small children, most of us are taught to be grateful for what we have. "Count your blessings" is such a common saying that it has become a permanent part of our everyday language. As children we were taught to say grace before dinner, and in response to our complaints about what was served for dinner, we were told we should be grateful that we weren't starving like the poor children of the world. When we complained too much about our life, we were admonished by our parents to be grateful for what we had instead of complaining about what we didn't have.

Most of us also had religious training that encouraged us to practice gratitude. So why do we have such a difficult time being grateful? Why is it so much easier to complain about what we don't have than it is to appreciate what we do? Are we just a perpetually ungrateful, greedy lot?

We are living in a time when it is difficult to be grateful. Many people are unemployed or struggling financially, and more and more are dying of AIDS, cancer and other diseases. Crimes are increasing, race relations are at an all-time low, and children are committing horrendous crimes at younger and younger ages. The environment is more polluted than ever, and we continue to destroy the rain forests. With all these problems and all this negativity, many people wonder, "What do we have to be grateful for?"

While the seeds of gratitude are often planted by parents and religion, our culture does not encourage these seeds to grow. We are bombarded with messages about what we should have, what we should strive for, what we should own. Until only recently, "More is better" was becoming more popular than "Count your blessings."

And in a culture that thrives on judgment, blame and scandal, it is easier to find fault in ourselves and in our lives than it is to be grateful for the good qualities of others and the positive aspects of their lives.

These seeds need to be nurtured, fed and cultivated. The key to cultivating a grateful spirit is in appreciating what we have instead of focusing on what we don't have. Richard Berendzen wrote the following about his experience:

> Inexplicably, I began to cherish my life. I told myself not to focus on what I had lost—my job, my identity—but on what I still had. I had my education, my family and my friends. I was outrageously healthy. I didn't have cancer or heart disease or AIDS. Certainly I had immense

problems, but they were finite and solvable. I had a future whenever I was ready to claim it. [1]

A grateful spirit:

- Helps us appreciate what we have
- Provides perspective
- Keeps us in the present
- Calms us down
- Helps us tolerate a situation until we can change it
- Helps us accept the things we cannot change
- Brings us closer to God
- Brings us closer to our loved ones
- Helps us raise happier, more successful children

Appreciating What You Have

One of the qualities that distinguishes the successful from so-called failures is the fact that they spend more time appreciating what they have than bemoaning what they do not. Christopher Reeve is a beautiful example of the power of gratitude. How can a man so crippled feel so fortunate? In a televised interview, he said, "Instead of obsessing about 'Why me?' and 'It's not fair,' I moved into 'What is the potential?' Now I can see opportunities and potentials I couldn't see before. Every moment means more."

Lili, the woman who was swindled by a con artist and had her heart broken and her reputation ruined in the process, also learned an important lesson.

---

[1] Berendzen, 65.

Lili

"My entire life changed because of the Mark incident," Lili told me. "Once I began to get over the humiliation of it all, I came to recognize that it was my vanity and my refusal to accept aging gracefully that got me into the mess I was in. There had been other men my own age who had asked me out before Mark, but I'd always turned them down. I'd tell myself, 'He's too old,' or 'He's bald,' or 'He's too fat.' I just didn't want to face the fact that *I* was getting old. I was flattered by Mark's attention and it helped me to stay in my fantasy world, pretending that I was still as young as I felt inside.

"Of course, I knew on some level that he was using me for money and prestige. I wasn't stupid, after all. But I fooled myself into thinking he really cared about me, too. I rationalized that there were plenty of women my age who'd love to entertain him. He could have his pick of women, but he chose *me*. But looking back on it now, I see how much I was deluding myself. He didn't care a thing about me. Most women my age would have sent him packing.

"This whole thing forced me to take a good look at myself and start accepting the fact that I was getting older. Through it all, I've started focusing less on how I *look* and more on what's inside of me. I've found that I'm a pretty interesting person, after all. I've made some new friends and I appreciate immensely those friends who've stuck by me. I've even started dating some men my age from the club. I've learned to look past their bald heads and wrinkles to see the person inside—something, I must confess, I've never done in my life. All in all, I think the whole situation has made me a better person, and I am very grateful."

Putting Your Life in Perspective

It is difficult to maintain a grateful spirit when you feel defeated or when it looks like you have no hope of making things better. You may feel forsaken by God or the universe, and believe that there is really nothing to feel grateful about. But these are the times when it is important to think about what your creator really has done for you. Although it may be difficult, think about how much worse it *could* be. For example, if you've lost your business and your house due to financial problems, think of how much worse it would be if you'd also lost your spouse and children, or if you'd become critically ill. This isn't denial or Pollyanna, pie-in-the-sky thinking. It's still important to face what you have to face. But it puts things in perspective. It humbles you and reminds you that you do, in fact, have something to be grateful for. It can also bring you back to God and renew your faith in the universe. You haven't been forsaken after all.

1. Think back to the previous year. How is your life better today than it was then? Write down all the ways you can think of.
2. Now go back two years. How is your life better than it was two years ago?
3. Do the same for five years.

Some of you may immediately say to yourself, "My life isn't any better. I have less money than I had a year ago. I'm older and less attractive than I was five years ago." Part of learning to have a grateful spirit is to look beneath the surface of things, to focus on the deeper meaning of things. Focus on other aspects of your life, on those things that have more significance, such as relationships, personal growth, spirituality. For example, are you and your partner closer than you were one year ago? Do you feel you are a better person than you were two years ago? Have you learned to slow down and appreciate your children more than you were able to five years ago?

Rachel

Rachel, the young woman who had her heart set on being an actress but went back to her hometown feeling defeated, learned that being grateful for what she had helped put her life in better perspective.

"The blessings from my fall weren't anything that dramatic. But all the same, it was a terrible humiliation for me to have to return to my hometown a 'failure' and to have to give up my dream.

"Talk about a life out of balance. Before I came home, I had no life outside of acting. I never dated because I didn't have time for a relationship. And I hardly ever met anyone except for other struggling actors who were as depressed and caught up in themselves as I was. Back home I started getting together with old friends after work and I made lots of new friends. I started appreciating the little things in life again. You know—a beautiful sunset, winter's first snow, wildflowers in a meadow. I realized how much I missed living in a small town, away from all the traffic and crime and smog. And I even started dating.

"After a while I decided to go back to school to become a teacher. I was lucky because my parents helped me out, but I didn't have it easy. I held down a part-time job the entire time I was in school. But nothing was as stressful as waitressing and auditioning all the time."

In a recent letter, Rachel told me she now teaches English, directs her school's senior play each year and acts as advisor for the drama club. She's also active in the local theater, and she's discovered she doesn't have to be on Broadway or in the movies to enjoy acting. She's involved with a wonderful man and they're thinking about getting married next year. She ended her letter with, "All in all I'd say I'm pretty blessed, wouldn't you?"

Prayers of Gratitude

One way to cultivate a grateful spirit is to begin each morning with a prayer of gratitude.

Thankful may I ever be for everything that God
    bestows.
Thankful for the joys and sorrows, for the blessings
    and the blows.
Thankful for the wisdom gained through
    hardships and adversity.
Thankful for the undertones as well as for the
    melody.
Thankful may I ever be for benefits both great and
    small—
and never fail in gratitude for that divinest gift of all:
the love of friends that I have known in times of fail-
    ures and success.

O may the first prayer of the day be always one of thankfulness.

PATIENCE STRONG

You may have already begun to recognize some of the blessings that have come from your fall. If you haven't, take heart. They will soon become evident. It is often difficult to recognize our blessings while in the midst of a crisis. As time passes and you begin to heal from your wounds, you will be able to look back at the situation and see it from a far different perspective.

PART IV

RISING FROM YOUR FALL

Forgiveness and Self-Acceptance

Misfortunes one can endure—
they come from outside, they are accidents.
But to suffer for one's own faults—ah
—there is the sting of life.

OSCAR WILDE

I dreamt last night,
of marvelous error,
that there were honeybees in my heart,
making honey out of my old failures.

ANTONIO MACHADO

Even though others may be slow to forgive you, you must work toward forgiving yourself for your fall, the things you did to create your fall, and the pain your fall caused others.

While true guilt and healthy shame can serve the positive function of discouraging you from repeating mistakes, holding on to your guilt and shame does nothing positive. If you have learned from your mistakes and are determined not to repeat them, then you no longer need your guilt. Let it go. Guilt can cause you to be self-destructive; abuse your body with food, alcohol, drugs, cigarettes; be accident-prone; sabotage your future success; or elicit punishment from others.

It is important for you to remember that you had reasons for doing whatever it was that you did that created your fall. This doesn't mean you should excuse what you did, but that you view it with the compassion and understanding you might give someone else with a similar background and history.

Lewis Smedes outlines the following steps to forgiving yourself:

- Hold yourself accountable for what you did.
- Give up your need to punish yourself.
- Revise your understanding of yourself. Remember that humans have faults and weaknesses. Work on gaining compassion for yourself to balance your judgment of yourself.
- Revise your feelings about yourself. You are a responsible person who failed, but you are also a worthy person who is accepted by God just the way you are.

- Try to become more accepting of yourself.[1]

Before you can rid yourself of guilt, you may need to atone for what you have done. It is important to be accountable for your actions and behavior. Being accountable can take various forms:

- Admitting your transgression to yourself and the person you hurt or damaged.
- Apologizing to the person (or persons) you hurt.
- Making amends or restitution.

We'll discuss more about taking responsibility and making amends in the next chapter.

Forgiveness also requires us to give up our ideas of being better or worse than others and to finally see ourselves as equals and co-learners. In the process of forgiveness, we transform the suffering we created by our own mistakes into psychological and spiritual growth.

There is a Buddhist idea that suffering exists specifically to teach us compassion. This idea can help you to face your actions so that you can forgive yourself for the hurts you have caused other people and forgive them for the hurts they have caused you.

Kahlil Gibran wrote about forgiveness in *The Prophet:*

Then one of the judges of the city stood forth and said,
  Speak to us of Crime and Punishment.
And he answered, saying:

---

[1] Smedes, 143-144.

It is when your spirit goes wandering upon the wind,
That you, alone and unguarded, commit a wrong unto
   others and therefore unto yourself.
And for that wrong committed must you knock and wait
   a while unheeded at the gate of the blessed.

Like the ocean is your god-self;
It remains for ever undefiled.
And like the ether it lifts but the winged.
Even like the sun is your god-self;
It knows not the ways of the mole nor seeks it the holes
   of the serpent.
But your god-self dwells not alone in your being.
Much in you is still man, and much in you is not yet man. [2]

What a wonderful way of talking about crime and punishment. Gibran's poem is far too long to include in its
entirety here, but I encourage you to read it. It sums up
what this chapter is all about: self-forgiveness ("Like the
ocean is your god-self; It remains for ever undefiled"); the
vulnerability and fallibility of human beings ("But your
god-self dwells not alone in your being. / Much in you is
still man, and much in you is not yet man."); judging others for their wrongdoing ("Oftentimes have I heard you
speak of one who commits a wrong as though he were
not one of you, but a stranger unto you and an intruder
upon your world. / But I say that even as the holy and
the righteous cannot rise beyond the highest which is in
each one of you, / So the wicked and the weak cannot
fall lower than the lowest which is in you also.").

---

[2] Kahlil Gibran, *The Prophet* (New York: Alfred A. Knopf, 1923), 39.

As I mentioned earlier, many people, at the moment of near-death, experience an instantaneous life review. Many would say this occurs so that their life can be judged and it can be determined whether they go to heaven or hell. Some believe it is so their creator can decide whether they are to return to earth again, and if so, in what form. But others believe it is to allow them to appreciate what they have learned and what remains to be learned. During their life review, people report being surrounded by the light of forgiveness and knowing that they are forgiven by their creator. The question is whether they can forgive themselves.

Once again we return to Dannion Brinkley's book, *Saved by the Light:*

> I looked at the Being of Light and felt a deep sense of sorrow and shame. I expected a rebuke, some kind of cosmic shaking of my soul. I had reviewed my life and what I had seen was a truly worthless person. What did I deserve if not a rebuke?
>
> As I gazed at the Being of Light I felt as though he was touching me. From that contact I felt a love and joy that could only be compared to the nonjudgmental compassion that a grandfather has for a grandchild. "Who you are is the difference that God makes," said the Being. "And that difference is love." There were no actual words spoken, but this thought was communicated to me through some form of telepathy.
>
> Again I was allowed a period of reflection. How much love had I given people? How much love had I taken from them? From the review I had just had, I could see that for every good event in my life, there were 20 bad

ones to weigh against it. If guilt were fat, I would have weighed 500 pounds.

As the Being of Light moved away, I felt the burden of this guilt being removed. [3]

Forgiving Yourself

The following visualization exercise is based on an ancient Chinese oracle—the *I Ching*. It will help you to begin to remove your burden of guilt and shame and move toward self-forgiveness.

- Find a quiet, comfortable place to sit or lie down.
- Begin breathing deeply and clearing your mind of all superfluous thoughts.
- As you continue breathing, visualize your harsh and unforgiving feelings to be carried away by the song of the flute, the reverberation of a drum, or the sound of the wind through the trees.
- In your mind's eye, see where the flow of positive energy is blocked, and then imagine this place as an ice floe breaking up in a thawing river.

All people make mistakes and you are no different. You don't need to continue to be critical of yourself, to suffer or punish yourself. You *do* need to learn from your mistakes, to be accountable for your behavior and to forgive yourself. In the next chapter we will focus on how to begin to take responsibility for your actions as part of

---

[3] Brinkley, 10.

resurrecting your reputation. This will, in turn, also help you to continue working toward self-forgiveness. By forgiving yourself you will gain the courage to face others, make restitution if need be and seek the forgiveness of those you have hurt.

Self-Acceptance

The way to heal your shame is through self-acceptance. Lewis Smedes, who wrote both *Shame and Grace* and *Forgive and Forget* (two books that have become classics on these subjects, and books that I recommend highly), believes that forgiving ourselves paves the road to self-acceptance.

> We forgive ourselves for the things we did. We accept ourselves as the persons we are. When we forgive ourselves, we heal our guilt; when we accept ourselves, we heal our shame. [4]

As Smedes states, accepting ourselves is an act of taking ownership of ourselves. Taking ownership implies that there is more to accepting ourselves than just feeling good about ourselves. He suggests four ways we can begin to take this ownership, three of which I will discuss here:

1. By owning what he calls our "raw material"
    We are all born with certain advantages and disadvantages. We inherit certain genes that determine to some degree not only our physical characteristics but also our emotional ones. We are further

---

[4] Smedes, 143.

influenced by the environment in which we are reared and the way we are treated by those around us, most particularly our parents and other caretakers.

Accepting ourselves requires us to accept our raw materials—our so-called good and so-called bad qualities, whatever they may be—instead of trying to twist ourselves around into someone we are not, or wasting our energies raging against the fates for giving us such raw materials.

Self-acceptance at any level also depends in part on accepting your body as it is, not as it isn't. This requires that you learn to admire your body and revel in what it can do, rather than focusing on its imperfections or perceived flaws.

2. By owning our Shadow

We've already talked extensively about accepting our Shadow, but I would like to just say here, as a reminder, that unless we can own *every* aspect of ourselves, our so-called unacceptable as well as our acceptable qualities, we will never fully accept ourselves.

We do not have to feel good about our so-called bad qualities, impulses and thoughts, but we do need to acknowledge them, own them and respect them as part of the selves we are. As Lewis Smedes writes in *Grace and Shame:*

Grace gives us permission: If God accepts us whole, light, dark, and shadowed, he gives us permission to accept ourselves as whole.

Grace-based people dare to own any current, any drive, any sadness, any joy, any urge that might show up in their spiritual basements. They know that nothing in their conscious or unconscious selves can make them unacceptable to God. Grace makes self-knowledge bearable.[5]

3. By taking pride in the self we own

Pride is often considered the opposite of shame. Shame is our failure to live up to the image that significant others have expected of us and that we have thus expected of ourselves. When we feel pride, it is because we feel we have reached others' expectations. Both pride and shame are *other*-related. If pride is the flip side of shame, then *grandiosity* is the flip side of debilitating shame. As Smedes states it:

> Shame and pride are opposite feelings about ourselves. Shame—the feeling of being unworthy and unacceptable—is the loss of pride. As shame is healed, we find our pride again.[6]

Many of us were raised to believe that to be proud is to be arrogant and to invite trouble; thus, pride goeth before the fall. Christian teaching asserts that pride is the worst of the seven deadly sins. But as Smedes states, "the pride that comes after grace is a very different thing than the pride that comes before the fall."[7]

The pride that comes before the fall is what the Greeks called hubris. We call it arrogance. Arrogance is usually

---

[5] Smedes, 147.
[6] Ibid., 148.
[7] Ibid., 149.

born of shame. Shame-bound people often overcompensate by pretending they are better than anyone else. But the arrogant person never fully believes his own lies. He doubts his own pride and the more he doubts, the more arrogant he becomes.

But Smedes assures us that there is a healthy pride that comes with grace. Arrogance is pride without gratitude. Grace-based pride is based on gratitude. An arrogant person thinks he *is* God. A person with grace-based pride thanks his God or creator. [8]

The way to heal our shame is by accepting ourselves. This is not an easy task by any means. We are moving toward self-acceptance when we take responsibility for creating our lives from whatever raw materials we were given. We are certainly closer to self-acceptance when we own our dark side, or Shadow, and give up attempting the impossible—to be "all good." And most important, perhaps, we are only inches away from self-acceptance when we add to these tasks the practice of gratitude for who we are.

If you remain depressed for long periods of time, I once again encourage you to seek professional help. Clinical and abandonment depression do not just go away on their own. I also encourage you to seek some sort of spiritual solace, whether in the form of prayer, meditation or music.

And remember, nothing you have done or will ever do will cause your creator(s) to turn his (her) back on you. You did not fall from grace in God's eyes, only in your own and in the eyes of those around you.

---

[8] Smedes, 144-151.

Resurrecting
Your Reputation

Do not look where you fell,
but where you slipped.

AFRICAN PROVERB

Remember your past mistakes just
long enough to profit by them.

DAN MCKINNON

Why are some people able to redeem themselves after a fall while others cannot? What did Vanessa Williams and Richard Nixon do that O.J. and Michael Jackson have not? What determines whether someone is able to rise again? Is it the type of act that created the fall or the person's attitude and actions after the fall?

These are some of the questions I will address in this chapter. In addition, I will share with you some "do's" and "don't's" concerning how to resurrect your damaged image or reputation.

First of all, it is very important that you not blame others, get caught up in self-pity or stay stuck in denial about your role in the fall. One of the great blessings that can come from a fall is in coming clean and telling the truth about the situation, and in essence, getting a whole new start.

Both O.J. Simpson and Michael Jackson are good examples of how not to go about resurrecting your image. Both present themselves as victims, refuse to admit any wrongdoing, and continue to appear arrogant and unrepentant. Michael Jackson continues to surround himself with children. Both show a marked lack of empathy toward the real victims. Whatever your opinion about their guilt or innocence, it is clear they have not learned their lessons from their fall.

You cannot resurrect your image if you do any of the following.

- Be self-pitying.
- Continue to deny or minimize what you did.

- Lie about what happened.
- Make excuses for what you did.
- Blame others for what happened.
- Continue the same behavior that contributed to your fall in the first place.
- Present yourself as a victim.
- Show a lack of empathy for the real victims.

In order to resurrect your image or reputation, you will need to be willing to do all of the following.

1. Take complete and utter responsibility for your fall, including apologizing to all those you hurt, disappointed or damaged and making restitution whenever possible.
2. Be willing to listen to the anger, hurt and disappointment of those affected by your fall.
3. Get help for the problems that caused your fall and complete unfinished business from the past.
4. Begin acting in ways that show your good intentions.

Taking Complete and Utter Responsibility for Your Fall

In addition to telling your friends and family about your fall, you must take complete responsibility for it. This means not blaming anyone else or making excuses for your actions. In addition, you will need to become accountable for your actions in the following ways.

- Admit to yourself that what you did was wrong, regardless of what led you to do it. Again, taking responsibility is different from blaming or chastising yourself.
- Make an apology to all those you hurt or damaged in any way. Ideally, this should be a face-to-face apology, but if that is not possible, a letter or phone call will do. The important thing is that you admit what you did, acknowledge the damage it may have caused others and show that you are sincere.
- Make restitution in the best way possible to any person who was hurt or damaged. This may mean financial restitution. For example, offer to pay for the therapy of the person you hurt or damaged, or offer to do some work for the person who lost money because of your actions.

Listening to the People Affected by Your Fall

Your family and friends (and anyone else affected by your fall) desperately need you to listen as they tell you how you hurt, betrayed, frightened or angered them by your actions. While this certainly won't be easy, it will be one of the most beneficial things you can do for those you've hurt and for yourself. It will help your loved ones to purge themselves of the anger, pain, fear, shame or disappointment that has plagued them. And it will help you take responsibility for what you did.

Getting Help for the Problems
That Led to Your Fall

Learn from your mistakes so that you will not repeat them. Seek therapy so that you will not continue on the same path that caused your fall. Join a 12-Step program to help you with addictions or compulsive behavior. Make a commitment to yourself to discover the cause of your fall and work actively to assure that you will not repeat the same mistakes.

Another way of taking responsibility for your fall is to clear up issues from your past or whatever it was that caused your fall. You must take a good hard look at your interactions with others and take responsibility for your part in relationship difficulties. This may mean seeking therapy to clear up unfinished business from your childhood, and it probably means learning how to express your anger.

If it has become clear to you that one of the reasons for your behavior and your fall was that you were victimized or neglected as a child, you will need to work on releasing your anger in constructive ways. Having been victimized or neglected creates tremendous rage inside a person. Since it is likely that you weren't able to release your anger at your abuser, that anger has probably festered and grown with every passing day.

Some victims turn their anger in on themselves rather than risk expressing it outwardly, which may cause a multitude of problems, including low self-esteem, depression, a belief that they deserved the abuse and a feeling that they do not deserve good things in their lives.

Having been victimized themselves, some victims may vent their anger on someone smaller and less powerful than themselves. Or they may select those who are more helpless and dependent in an attempt to protect themselves from the humiliation of the abuse, or to feel as powerful as their oppressor. Since they hated themselves for being weak and helpless, they grow to hate others who are weak as well. This behavior may have begun in childhood and continued into adulthood.

Victims need to learn constructive ways of ventilating their anger so that they will not carry it around or turn it against themselves or others. By ventilating your anger, you will learn to place responsibility for previous abuse or neglect where it belongs, experience a feeling of empowerment and learn that your anger is nothing to be feared.

Beginning to Act in Ways That Show Your Good Intentions

The best way to resurrect your image or reputation and regain the trust and confidence of those you have hurt is to act in ways that show you have every intention of being a better person in the future.

One way of doing this is to take your focus away from your self-involved, egocentric self and place it instead on cooperation, service, the cultivation of relationships and empathy toward others.

Focus on the values of health, truthfulness, self-respect, courage. As Marsha Sinetar, in *Elegant Choices, Healing Choices* wrote:

The elegant choice consists of our motivation to move in a healthful, helpful, life-supporting direction as well as it consists of our actual choice or action. Whether we are ready to take one step or many matters less than our general direction of motives and choices. Which way are we headed? Toward health and wholeness, or toward self-pity, withdrawal, neuroticism and malfunction? What do we say to ourselves when we see we are stuck? Do we allow ourselves human emotion and fallibility or demand robust participation even during a crisis?

What heals us, what begins our self-renewal—thus, I believe, promoting actualization—can be just some tiny act. We are simply required to do what we can do, here and now, at this moment in time. Even the right thought can help if we're too discouraged, too exhausted, to act. The mere flick of an eye in the elegant direction, coupled with our intent to bring our more whole self into being, begins our gradual move into more productive ways of choosing. [1]

The following are some suggestions for elegant choices you can make to help resurrect your image or reputation.

- Reach out to the victims of your fall and try to help them in any way you can. If you cannot help them directly, help others who are in similar circumstances.
- Get involved in a charity that helps the poor, the disadvantaged or the sick.
- If you are a celebrity, a politician or other public figure, take a break from the spotlight. Let things cool

---

[1] Sinetar, 17-18.

off before appearing in public or before getting involved in highly visible activities.

Doing good works, getting involved with causes and helping those around you are certainly good ways of resurrecting your reputation. But these actions on your part need to come from your heart, and not be a way of impressing others.

The very best way to resurrect your reputation is to make a commitment to yourself to live your life with honesty, integrity and compassion for others. This is far more important than reviving your image. If you have learned from your fall and have changed from the inside out, make no mistake about it: people will notice.

A Second Chance

There is no need to live the rest of your life regretting what you've done in the past, wishing things had been different, or living in a world of "if only's." While it is important to always remember the lessons of your fall, now is the time to move forward instead of looking back.

You are likely a better person than you were before your fall. You are probably less arrogant and more humble, less judgmental and more empathetic, less critical and more forgiving.

Now is the time to take your lessons and blessings and make something far more positive out of your life and the lives of the people around you. Having survived your fall and reaped the benefits of its many blessings, you now have a second chance at life. Whether your fall was a moral, financial or physical one, you now have the opportunity to live the rest of your life as a healthier, wiser, more caring person. Few people get a second chance at life. Your fall has afforded you this unique opportunity. Use it wisely.

PART V

WHEN A LOVED ONE FALLS FROM GRACE

As I mentioned in chapter 1, this book is not just for those who have experienced a fall. It is also for those who have been hurt by the fall of someone they love or admire. If you haven't already done so, I suggest you read the first four parts of this book. While the information there is not directed toward you, it will give you important insight into the mind and emotions of the person who has fallen, and this, in turn, will benefit you.

There have been hundreds of people who have been hurt by the fall from grace of their favorite teacher, spiritual leader, doctor or family member. How do you cope when someone you have loved, admired, depended upon is one of these people? How do you work to recover your trust, and what can you learn from the experience? The next three chapters are devoted to answering these questions.

19

Coping with Your Shame and Anger

The person who experiences a fall from grace is not the only one to be humiliated and shamed by the experience.

Maureen

"When my daughter was accused of killing Kimberly, it was more than I could take. We were already devastated by the loss of our grandchild. Then when the police started steering the investigation toward my daughter, we were nearly destroyed.

"Instead of people sympathizing with us, they became angry with us and accused us of being bad parents who raised a killer for a daughter. When we stood

> by Pamela, we were accused of being in denial, of being
> blind to the truth.
>
> "People in our town started ostracizing us. We'd walk
> past people who'd been our friends for years and they'd
> completely ignore us. It was humiliating."

As a loved one of someone who has fallen, you will
no doubt suffer incredible shame and anger. You may
feel humiliated and angry if your loved one has been
publicly exposed and/or chastised; you may suffer from
the shame of having to live a lesser lifestyle; and you
may feel guilt and shame by association—if my mother
is guilty of this, what does it say about me? Family and
friends of the fallen need help to handle all these
feelings.

It is very important that you learn how to support your
loved one without going "down the tubes" with that person. For example, when a child does something the community considers shameful, it is common for parents to
take the child's shame on themselves.

You need to separate yourself from the fallen person.
You are not the guilty party or guilty by association, and
you did not cause that person's fall, no matter what the
circumstances. Refer to chapter 2 for help in understanding more about shame and how it works.

Expressing Your Anger

More than likely, you will have a lot of anger toward the
person who fell. You'll be angry that he got into this mess,
made errors in judgment, was so reckless with his life and

yours, and that you weren't given a clue about what was going on.

You have a right to your anger and a right to express that anger. My suggestion is that you make sure you release your anger constructively and that if you choose to confront the fallen person directly, that you pick the right time to do so.

For example, if the person who has fallen is seriously depressed, even suicidal, it is obviously not the right time to vent your anger. Instead, find a constructive way of releasing your anger in a more indirect way. You can choose to write your feelings down or have an imaginary conversation in which you express all your feelings toward the person who has fallen.

If you recognized your partner, child, parent or friend when I described the narcissistic personality earlier in the book, you will need to take extra precautions when confronting him with your anger. It is vitally important that you realize that no matter how much bravado a person with narcissistic tendencies may exhibit, it is a false facade. Underneath that bravado lies a person who is extremely insecure and sensitive, so sensitive that he cannot tolerate criticism of any kind. Criticism and judgment feel like mortal blows to a person suffering from narcissism or narcissistic tendencies. Therefore, keep this in mind when you talk with him. Be honest about your anger, but don't be surprised if he defends himself against it with denial or anger. Until he receives some serious help, in the form of therapy or a 12-Step program, he cannot help but respond in this automatic, habitual way. It does not necessarily mean he is not hearing you or not agreeing with you. It is just that his ego is so fragile, he may not be able to let you know.

Since the narcissist is so good at presenting the illusion of having it all, there is a natural tendency to envy him and a certain delight in seeing him fall. We enjoy watching the narcissist get his due or reveal that he is not immune to frustration or pain. The narcissist cannot share the joke because he cannot admit his vulnerabilities. He will only get more defensive if you try to get him to admit them or to laugh about them.

It is important for you to feel and express your anger and not get stuck in blame. Holding on to anger and blame causes people to grow bitter, as their anger eats away at them like a cancer. They become obsessed with trying to find a way to make the person who hurt them pay for what he has done. Their lives become swallowed up with their need for revenge as they give the person who hurt them an undue amount of power over them.

Jack

Although Jack has been legally divorced from his ex-wife, Rebecca, for a year and a half, he has not emotionally divorced her. He hasn't gotten over the fact that Rebecca left him for another man and caused him to feel humiliated by his friends and family. While it is easy to see why Jack would be angry and hurt by his ex-wife's actions, it is more difficult to understand why he doesn't let go. His anger, instead of dissipating as time goes by, seems to be increasing. He talks to anyone who will listen about how victimized he feels by Rebecca, what a bitch she is, and how he wishes she were dead. Jack may have been victimized by his wife's abandonment, but now he is victimized by his own inability to let go of his rage and go on with his life.

It is your responsibility to acknowledge and release your feelings of shame and anger concerning the fall. In chapter 21 we will examine further this responsibility and how to deal with these emotions.

How to Support Those Who Have Fallen

When we treat a man as he is,
we make him worse than he is. When we
treat him as if he is already what he
potentially could be, we make
him what he should be.

Family and friends of the fallen have a tremendous amount of power when it comes to either helping or adding to the burden of their loved one. They can either help the individual to learn lessons or make it harder to see the light. In this chapter I will offer suggestions on how to be supportive without diminishing the fallen person's chances for a new beginning.

For example, I advise you *not* to shore up the person who has fallen by giving false hope and making false promises (i.e., saying you are going to stay married when you plan to divorce as soon as the crisis has passed). The person who has fallen *needs* to face the truth at this time—the truth about herself *and* her relationships.

Some people, especially narcissistic personalities, *need* to crumble, to fall apart in order to make significant changes. In Alcoholics Anonymous this is referred to as "hitting bottom." If you shore them up, you actually prevent them from facing the truth about themselves and from hitting bottom so they can rise out of the ashes.

Don't do that to your loved one. Don't take away this chance for redemption. Don't rob him of his dignity and integrity by encouraging him to lie to protect you or himself.

In the case of a scandal, be honest with yourself, take your head out of the sand and be open to the strong possibility that he did do that of which he is accused. We are all capable of cruel, selfish, immoral acts. No one is all good. Work at seeing your loved one for who he is, not just as who you want him to be. Tell him you are strong enough to hear the truth and that you want to hear it. Then keep your mouth shut and let him tell it. Don't interrupt him by saying things like, "I know you didn't mean to do it," or, "Oh, it wasn't *that* bad." Don't overprotect him by hugging him while he is trying to talk. And don't overreact by crying and questioning him with,

"Oh my God, how could you?" All these actions on your part will stop him from opening up and pouring out his heart to you, which is what you both desperately need.

Support the fallen by being honest with them; by assuring them you will stand by as they own up to their mistakes (if they are true), and telling them you respect them when they do.

Dealing with a Narcissistic Personality

If you've discovered in reading the first four parts of the book that the person who experienced the fall is most likely a narcissistic personality or seems to have some of these tendencies, you may now be viewing that person through different eyes. You may suddenly be keenly aware of the fact that he seems to be continually wrapped up in himself and the things he is involved in, and that he seldom asks you about yourself. You may suddenly be struck by his seeming lack of empathy for others, or wonder whether he is manipulating you in order to get what he wants. This kind of suspicion and leeriness can create a tremendous wedge between you and the person who has fallen.

It is important to remember that people suffering from a narcissistic personality disorder cannot help who they are any more than if they had any other type of personality disorder or mental illness. They are not just being selfish, egocentric people because they *want* to. It is not a matter of choice.

Once people who suffer from this disorder are confronted with the truth about themselves, as I hope this book will serve to do, they are often mortified at their own behavior. Perhaps for the first time in their life, they are able to see themselves clearly—and they probably won't like what they see. This new awareness, coupled with the humiliation from their fall, can cause them to work hard on being a different kind of person. If this is what happened to your loved one, if you have seen any attempt on her part to change, please be patient. It takes a lot for people to admit this about themselves; to humble themselves in this way.

It will also take a lot of work on their part to change. Unless they have gone into long-term analysis in order to rebuild and restructure their personalities, the changes will be superficial at first. They will have to constantly catch themselves in the act of being selfish, monopolizing the conversation, being superficial, etc. Through much effort, the changes will become a part of their personality, but this will take time.

Support your loved one in the ways I have suggested, but keep in mind that *you* also need support. The person who has fallen may not be able to give you the support you need at this time, so you may need to reach out to friends, family or health-care professionals. Do not hesitate to seek this help. You are going through a trauma as surely as if you were the person who fell.

Your Lessons
and Blessings

And why beholdest thou the mote
that is in thy brother's eye, but considerest not
the beam that is in thine own eye?

MATTHEW 7:2-3.

We are often reborn or re-created by our tragedies. In fact, it often takes a crisis or tragedy to mold us into the person we were meant to be all along. Why does this so often occur? Is it that tragedy strips away all the superfluous aspects of our personalities and reveals our basic nature—whether strong or weak, virtuous or exploitive? Or can it be likened to alchemy—a new self being created from the fires of tragedy?

One of the definitions of the word *crisis* is "turning point." The Chinese define it as "opportunity." In this chapter, I will focus on the lessons that can be learned from having a loved one fall from grace.

For example, the most crucial turning point in Eleanor Roosevelt's life was her reaction to finding letters that revealed her husband's affair with Lucy Mercer. Devastated by the discovery, she offered Franklin a divorce. But surprisingly, her heretofore rival—her mother-in-law, Sara Delano Roosevelt—came down squarely on Eleanor's side and threatened to cut her son off without a penny if he left his family.

Eleanor responded initially by becoming afflicted with anorexia and by often responding in the passive/ aggressive style she called her "patient Griselda" mode —marked, as it was, by the long-suffering so highly recommended to women in Western culture.

But Eleanor learned at last to reach beyond betrayal and a dour response to create a binding, if unconventional, partnership with her husband. Together they would leave a lasting impact on American minds, souls and institutions as well as on women's sense of the possible.

In the time following her turning point, Eleanor discovered her dazzling gifts as a teacher, became a syndicated columnist, a ready speaker, a political organizer and a tactician of real genius. For the rest of her life, Eleanor was often brilliant, sometimes cold, from time to time inept, frequently baffled, on occasion deeply hurt, but always working her way toward greater clarity of mind and generosity of spirit.

It may turn out that your blessings from the fall come from a renewed closeness with your partner, your child or whomever it was that experienced a fall. As you know, crises can often bring people closer together, and a fall from grace is no exception. Weathering the storm together may have caused you to band together toward a common goal, or may have opened up the lines of communication long closed from neglect and time.

On the other hand, a fall from grace can also tear people apart. While you may have been willing to stand by your spouse, lover or friend while going through the crisis, you may find that his act is something you simply cannot tolerate, understand or accept. This is especially true if you have not seen much remorse from him, or if the person does not appear to have learned from the experience. As painful as ending a relationship can be, it can also be a blessing in disguise. Perhaps now it is time for you to end an empty or abusive relationship, to face your own issues and ultimately get a new start on life.

Instead of focusing all your attention on deciding whether the fallen has learned his or her lesson, you need to focus on your own. Having someone you love or admire fall from grace can be an incredible opportunity for you to learn some wonderful lessons as well.

These are examples of the lessons that can be learned.

1. Don't put anyone up on a pedestal. Open your eyes to see the real person instead of holding onto

a fantasy about him. Don't be blinded by charm, false promises, etc.

2. Don't allow envy to blind you to your own talents and good qualities.

3. Don't give your power away to anyone.

4. Own your own Shadow personality, or dark side.

5. Learn to be less judgmental and more empathetic.

6. Practice forgiveness.

Removing Them from Their Pedestals

Men will never disappoint us if we
observe two rules: (1) To find out what they are;
(2) To expect them to be just that.

GEORGE ILES

Be not swept off your feet by the
vividness of the impression, but say,
'Impression, wait for me a little. Let me see what you
are and what you represent.
Let me try you.'

EPICTETUS

Those who enjoyed the anonymity and protection of previous eras are now being exposed in record numbers. It is impossible to pick up the newspaper without learning of another priest, therapist, politician or entertainer who has abused the trust placed in him or her. In fact, it has been said that our new national pastime is humbling our heroes. Cultural icons—from the Roosevelts and the Kennedys to Walt Disney and Michael Jackson—are being scrutinized and unmasked.

We all have paid a high price for placing those in the public eye on pedestals. By expecting them to be superhuman in their thoughts and actions, we not only make their fall inevitable but also stunt our own ability to be compassionate. While sometimes we do need to blow the whistle in order to stop illegal and immoral actions, we also need to be aware that everyone who makes a mistake—even quite a bad mistake—is not necessarily a bad person. Learning what lies beneath our desire to point fingers and assign blame is important, as only by forgiving others their mistakes can we learn how to forgive ourselves.

And by placing others on a pedestal, we negate our own worth. By idealizing others, we devalue ourselves.

Stop Letting Envy Blind You to Your Own Talents

Beware of envy: For to grudge any
man an advantage in person and fortune
is to censure the liberality of providence,
and to be angry at the
goodness of God.

GEORGE SHELLEY

Grudge not another what you
cannot attain yourself.

ENGLISH PROVERB

Envy is an emotion that we all feel but only a few understand. We seldom hear it talked about and very little has been written about it. But envy does exist and it works its destruction all the more powerfully because we refuse to face it.

What exactly is envy? It is our longing for what another person has. It is when we ache for the possessions, position and perceived happiness of others.

Envy and jealousy are often confused. In envy we seek to defeat our rival, not out of love for the third party to whom we both lay claim, but because we begrudge our rival anything we cannot possess. By contrast, in jealousy we aim to possess the beloved and to get rid of the rival. Jealousy is clearly a three-person relationship, whereas envy concerns only two: the envied and the envier. Jealousy is founded on love for the whole person, whereas envy reduces the other to a part it wants to ruin if it cannot be appropriated.

When we envy someone, we not only want what the other person has but feel that, by rights, what they have belongs to us. In our minds it is almost as if the other person stole from us the very things we envy.

It is very common for the mates, siblings, friends and even the children of successful, powerful, attractive people to envy them. Even though you may personally benefit from the fame or success of someone you love, it is often difficult not to hate their joy and prosperity if you aren't achieving your own goals.

The reason we are often consumed with envy is because we do not believe we will ever gain what the envied has. We are consumed with envy of their good because we despair of ever gaining it. The great tragedy is that our envy blinds us to the good that is inside of ourselves. Our own unique gifts and talents are lost to us. We see our own neglected talents in others, and that is why we feel others have taken from us.

The way past envy is not to ignore it, but to embrace it and learn its message. In actuality, envy is a rejection of the good things within ourselves. The envious person avoids the human potential to individuate (prepare for a career, hone a talent).

When we envy someone we are attempting to get off the hook of our struggle with ourselves. But envy *can* lead us to what needs repair in our identities. Envy, so spoiling and injurious, can, if suffered consciously, point us toward the good we thirst for.

Taking Back Your Power

In the process of your loved one's fall, you may have learned that you have been in an unequal relationship. As I mentioned earlier, any good relationship—whether with your mate, a friend or a coworker—is a relationship of equals. This means that both parties contribute equally to the relationship (even if this is done in entirely different ways), and each person values the other's contributions.

In addition, each has an equal say in making decisions and each takes responsibility for his own actions.

If you suspect that you have been in an unequal relationship but aren't sure, take the test on page 100 in chapter 8. If you've answered "my partner" (or friend, or coworker) to most of the questions, you have probably been in an unequal relationship and may have allowed this person to control or even abuse you.

If you are in a relationship with someone who devalues you, looks down on you and doesn't recognize your worth, then there may be little or no hope for the relationship unless both of you change substantially. Ask yourself these questions:

- Does this person see me as an equal?
- Does he have a general attitude of being superior to me?
- Do I believe this person is superior to me?

If you answered "no" to the first question or "yes" to either or both of the other two, you are in an unequal relationship, and you are being devalued by the other person and/or you are devaluing yourself. To discover how each of you honestly feels about your own and the other's innate value, complete the following exercise:

1. Make a list of all the ways you feel that you contribute to the relationship (for example, emotional support, child care, money, social skills, special talents, maintenance of the house or yard, responsibility for the family budget). In a separate room or location, have the other person do the same.

2. After completing this list, make a list of the ways in which you feel the other person contributes to the relationship.
3. Still by yourself, look over your own lists and draw whatever conclusions you can. Is one of the lists substantially longer than the other?
4. Now exchange lists and compare how the two of you perceive the situation.

This exercise can be very revealing. It can help you both to see the other person's point of view—*if* you are both open to learning and can approach the experience in a non-defensive way. The other person may be surprised to realize that you contribute so much and may therefore be able to change his image of you and value you more.

The opposite can also be true, of course. The other person may argue that the things you contribute are not all that important or are things that are merely expected in a relationship; or he may otherwise devalue the ways you contribute. If this is the case, you are in an unequal relationship.

Letting Go of Your Victim Mentality

If you feel victimized by the person who has fallen, it may be important for you to look closely at your personal history to discover whether you have a pattern of being victimized by others. Those who have been victimized in the past tend to continually see themselves as victims, to put themselves in situations where they will be victimized again, and to surround themselves with those who continue to victimize them.

Those who go from one abusive relationship to another must begin to recognize that while they do not cause another person to be emotionally, physically or sexually abusive, there are reasons why they keep choosing abusive people to be involved with. They need to take responsibility for discovering these reasons, especially when there are children involved.

Cristi

For example, Cristi's husband has recently become physically abusive. She doesn't want to leave him because he just lost his job and he has never hit her before. But Cristi realizes that when a man begins to abuse his wife, he usually doesn't stop. The reason she knows this so well is because she has been through it two other times. Twice before she listened when a man promised he wouldn't do it again, and twice before she stayed too long. This time Cristi is smart enough to leave, but leaving is only half the answer. Now Cristi must look at why she once again chose a violent man and what in her background set her up for such an attraction. Now she must make sure she never chooses a violent man again, for her sake and for the sake of her two children.

While you may not have been dominated, controlled or abused by the person who fell, you may have discovered you were betrayed or deceived. Realizing that someone you loved or cared about deeply has been lying to you, cheating on you, or living a double life can make you feel as much of a victim as domination or abuse.

The Tyranny of Innocence

You have a lot more power to change the course of your life than you realize. The way to get in touch with this power is by taking responsibility for yourself and your actions. By continuing to see yourself as a victim, by believing that you are always the damaged one, always the innocent one, and by believing that you can justify your behavior based on the fact that you have been victimized, you not only avoid taking responsibility for your life but take away your own power in the process.

There is indeed a tyranny in constantly viewing oneself as the innocent one, as the victim. It keeps you in a one-down position, robbing you of your personal power. It prevents you from recognizing the power you have and realizing your ability to make choices, thus preventing you from making changes within yourself that can improve your circumstances.

By remaining naive and childlike in your attitude (expecting life to be fair, people to have good reasons for their behavior, etc.), you not only invite abuse or dishonesty, but provide for yourself a cushion against having to face your anger and pain, and an excuse for not taking action.

Taking Responsibility

The best way to break out of a victim mentality is to get in touch with the power you do have and to exert this power. The most empowering way of doing this is for you to begin to take responsibility in the following ways:

1. Begin taking responsibility *for yourself.* This includes: not expecting others to take care of you; meeting your own needs; speaking up for your rights and needs; leaving abusive situations and relationships; and taking responsibility for your own recovery and healing, including seeking professional help when needed.

2. Take responsibility *for your anger.* Victims often hold on to their anger as a way of avoiding letting go or grieving their losses. You need to find constructive ways of releasing your anger so that you don't turn it back on yourself or get to the point of hurting someone else.

3. Take responsibility *for your own actions (or inaction)* and your own part in an interaction. Victims are often blind to the effect their own actions have on others.

4. Take responsibility *for your choices.* This includes taking a close look at with whom you choose to be involved with and at the reasons why you have chosen to stay in abusive relationships and situations.

Once these tasks are completed, the person who has been living life as a victim will cease to exist. In his place will be a stronger, wiser, more effective person capable of taking care of himself in ways never imagined.

The price you pay for not shouldering your own burdens is that you eventually lose the strength to hold yourself up. Ultimately, the price you pay to have some-one take care of you is your freedom.

With freedom comes responsibility and vice versa. There is a direct connection between our ability (or inability) to accept responsibility and the amount of con-trol we have over our life. For example, children are truly the only people who are not responsible for their actions, but children don't have much control over their lives, either. In fact, we could say that the amount of freedom a child experiences is in direct proportion to the amount of responsibility the child takes on. The more responsibility a child takes on, the more privileges he or she is given.

The same holds true for you. By being accountable for your behavior, by taking responsibility for your own life, you will gain the very freedom you envy in others, a freedom you never imagined possible.

Owning Your Own Shadow Personality, or Dark Side

There is no such thing as a totally innocent person. We all have the capacity to deceive, manipulate, use and abuse others. There is a part of ourselves we hide away not only from others but from ourselves. This dark side is made up of forbidden thoughts and feelings, undesir-able and thus rejected personality traits, and all the vio-lent and sexual tendencies we consider evil, dangerous or forbidden.

We often hide our dark side behind a mask of sweet-ness, innocence and fragility. While looking honestly at your own dark side may threaten you, it will also enlighten and empower you, and help you recognize your own tendency to dominate, control, abuse, hide and lie. You may have the very qualities that you find unacceptable or repulsive in the person who fell.

For example, your intolerance for the shallowness, self-centeredness and manipulative qualities of the narcissist may be a signal that you have buried or rejected these very qualities within yourself. In fact, the negative image we have of narcissism may indicate that self-preoccupation contains something we need so badly that it is surrounded by negative connotations.

Dr. Carl Jung, the famous psychoanalyst who first brought the importance of the Shadow, or dark side, to our attention, explained that when we feel repulsed by a quality or characteristic of another, it is because we are confronting something in ourselves that we find objectionable, something with which we ourselves struggle.

To encounter the elements of Shadow, we need to examine what traits, characteristics and attitudes we dislike in other people and how strongly we dislike them. The simplest method is to list all the qualities we do not like in other people—for instance, conceit, short temper, selfishness, bad manners and greed. When the list is finally complete (and it will probably be quite lengthy), we must extract those characteristics that we not only dislike in others but hate, loathe and despise. This shorter list will be a fairly accurate picture of our personal Shadow.

If you list selfishness, for example, as one of those traits in others that you simply cannot stand, and if you adamantly criticize the person who has fallen for selfishness in relating to people, you would do well to examine your own behavior to see if perhaps you, too, practice selfishness.

Of course, not all criticisms of others are projections of our own undesirable Shadow traits. But anytime our response to another person involves excessive emotions or overreaction, we can be sure that something unconscious has been prodded and is being activated. If Tom is sometimes selfish, for example, there is a certain degree of reasonableness about my offense at his behavior. But in true Shadow projection, my condemnation of Tom will far exceed his demonstration of the fault.

Becoming Less Judgmental and More Compassionate

There are many benefits to becoming more empathetic and compassionate versus being judgmental. For example:

1. Judging makes us pompous, self-righteous, hard-hearted. Empathy softens us; causes us to be open-hearted and wise; gives us depth; makes us fuller, more interesting people.
2. Judging makes us contract. It causes us to be small and narrow-minded. Empathy causes us to be expansive and open-minded.
3. Judging blinds us to others while empathy helps us to clearly see others—both their positive and negative qualities. It is like a magic telescope that helps us to see inside others, to view their heart and soul.

4. Judging separates us from others, while empathy connects us; empathy helps us to see our similarities, joining us in our humanity.

5. Judging makes us inaccessible to our children. It makes it difficult if not impossible for them to talk to us, trust us, come to us with their problems. Empathy makes us more accessible, more trustworthy, invites our children to confide in us and seek our advice and help.

6. Last but certainly not least, if we ever expect to change society, to lower the crime rate, to have an effect on the behavior of criminals, we *must* make it easier for criminals to *admit* when they have "sinned" and to ask for help. By being so judgmental, we encourage lawbreakers to lie and do whatever is necessary to avoid our judgments. We encourage them to blame others, to look for excuses for their behavior—anything to ward off our harsh judgments. Because we make them into monsters we rob them and ourselves of the chance to heal, forgive and be forgiven.

Working Past Your Black-and-White Thinking

Most of us tend to feel more comfortable with actions that seem clear-cut—good or bad, black or white. Ambiguity—the gray areas that characterize most of real life—makes us feel uncomfortable and unsettled. But no one is all good or all bad. We all combine good and bad qualities; we all share the capacity to do both good and evil.

Becoming less judgmental and more compassionate of others (and of ourselves) requires the ability to accept the range of grays that make us all human. We are each a composite, a mosaic of different thoughts, emotions and choices of behavior. All people are more mature in some areas than in others. Rather than thinking in terms of "good" and "bad," I encourage you to think in terms of conscious and unconscious, aware and unaware.

It is possible to be a wonderful parent *and* be impatient, to be kind *and* selfish, loving *and* occasionally judgmental, a nice person *and* angry at the same time. And no matter who we are and how hard we have worked to become whole and aware, we will still make mistakes. We need to accept our humanity and that of others, with all its imperfections.

In rejecting the tyranny of black-and-white thinking, we become less rigid, self-righteous, stuffy and judgmental and more flexible, accepting, spontaneous and loving.

Practicing Detachment

Having expectations of others that are unreasonable or too high is a primary cause of judgment. For this reason, we must work on letting go of these expectations and practicing detachment.

Many people believe that detachment means giving up on a person or a situation, no longer caring. But detachment is caring from a very deep yet objective place.

We know we are too attached to an outcome, a person, or the way we or another person should act if we:

- Insist on having our way
- Lose our sense of humor about the situation
- Have an intense emotional reaction or take an emotional position

Most of us need to lighten up, let go of some control and leave room for spontaneity. We need to become more objective and get our personal feelings out of the way. This does not mean we repress our emotions, but rather work with intent to be in a different place, to see things differently.

A major reason for expectations is our need to be in control. We most especially need to work on letting go of control in our relationships, especially with our children. If we are practicing detachment we do not need to judge, we do not need to overcontrol.

Practicing Acceptance

Acceptance is the opposite of judgment. Therefore, in order to become less judgmental, we must learn acceptance. When we accept others just the way they are, with all their faults and mistakes, we give them a wonderful, healing gift that can literally transform them and our relationship with them.

This doesn't mean we never get angry or never feel disappointed. It just means that we don't place conditions on our love for them.

Acceptance requires letting go of control, learning to trust, learning to surrender to what is. Self-surrender is a concept that is somewhat foreign to the Western mind, and yet, as a longing that lies deep within the heart, it may be hauntingly familiar.

Learning Forgiveness

Never criticize a man until you've
walked a mile in his moccasins.

AMERICAN INDIAN PROVERB

Whenever you start measuring
somebody, measure him right, child, measure him
right. Make sure you done taken into account what
hills and valleys he came
through before he got to whatever he is.

LORRAINE HANSBERRY

We are all teachers for one another. Without error on someone's part, none of us would learn the lesson of compassion that forgiveness brings. Even our enemies can reveal to us aspects of ourselves we have rejected and can tell us the truth about ourselves in ways that no one else can.

In the process of psychotherapy or personal spiritual growth, many people discover that what they originally thought was an evil event was really something quite positive. Many persons, for instance, frightened and overwhelmed at some breakdown in their lives, are forced to undergo powerful transformations in their personality that they later realize were good. They then view the original dark condition as a blessing, since it drove them to make the creative changes.

Forgiveness is not a self-righteous or Polyanna-like turning of the other cheek or a condoning of abhorrent behavior. But if we can understand the deep pain from which arose hurtful actions inflicted on us, then we have suffered with the other person; we have been compassionate. In that act of compassion, we move out of the role of victim and see beyond those actions to the heart of the person who is acting.

Forgiving is not the same as forgetting or excusing. These are completely different functions. For example, in forgiving a murderer by being compassionate and understanding the roots of his actions, we don't let him out of jail unless he is rehabilitated. In forgiving your loved one or friend for his fall and for the pain it has caused you, you need not overlook his action. But you are required to communicate about it.

To learn to forgive is to break with an unforgiving past. Forgiveness is such a gift that "give" lives in the word. Christian tradition has tried to make it a meek and passive word (i.e., turn the other cheek). But the word contains the active word "give," which reveals its truth: it involves the act of taking something of yours and handing it to another, so that from now on it is theirs. Nothing passive about it. It is an exchange—an exchange of faith, the faith that what has been done can be transcended. When two people need to make this exchange with each other, it can be one of the most intimate acts of their lives. Forgiveness is a promise to *work* at transcending.

Conclusion

M any blessings can be garnered by both those who have fallen from grace and their loved ones. I hope this book has given you hope and helped you to begin looking for the inevitable blessings that come from such a life-transforming experience.

It has been an honor sharing my knowledge and my own experience with you, and as usual, I have learned a great deal from doing it. God bless you.

Appendix I: Resources

American Association of Marriage and Family Therapy (AAMFT)

1717 K Street NW
Suite 407
Washington, DC 20006

Will refer you to a licensed marriage, family, child therapist in your area.

American Association of Sex Educators, Counselors and Therapists (AASECT)

11 Dupont Circle NW
Suite 220
Washington, DC 20036

Will refer you to an experienced, certified sex therapist in your area.

Childhelp USA

6463 Independence Avenue
Woodland Hills, CA 91367
Hotline: 800-4-A-CHILD or 800-422-4453

Provides comprehensive crisis counseling for adult and child victims of child abuse and neglect, offenders, parents who are fearful of abusing or who want information on how to be effective parents.

National Association for Perinatal Addiction Research and Education (NAPARE)

11 E. Hubbard St.
Suite 200
Chicago, IL 60611
(312) 329-2512

Provides a network for exchange of information and ideas regarding prevention and intervention in the problems caused by substance abuse during pregnancy.

National Clearinghouse for Alcohol and Drug Information (NCADI)

P.O. Box 2345
Rockville, MD 20850
(301) 468-2600

Gathers and disseminates information on alcohol- and drug-related subjects, produces public awareness materials on substance abuse prevention and distributes a wide variety of publications on alcohol and drug abuse.

National Institute of Justice Reference Service (NIJRS)

National Institute of Justice
P.O. Box 6000
1600 Research Blvd.
Rockville, MD 20850
800-851-3420

Provides information on all aspects of law enforcement and criminal justice, answers inquiries, distributes publications and makes referrals.

National Mental Health Association Prevention Clearinghouse

1021 Prince St.
Alexandria, VA 22314
(703) 684-7722

Offers a network to connect experts with those in need of assistance and to facilitate communication among professionals involved in primary prevention.

Parents United/Daughters and Sons United/Adults Molested as Children United

232 East Gish Road
San Jose, CA 95112
(408) 453-7616

Provides guided self-help for sexually abusive parents as well as child and adult victims of sexual abuse; 150 chapters nationwide.

VOICES (Victims of Incest Can Emerge Survivors) in Action, Inc.

P.O. Box 148309
Chicago, IL 60614
(312) 327-1500

A national network of female and male survivors and pro-survivors that has local groups and contacts throughout the country. Offers a free referral service that provides listings of therapists, agencies and self-help groups.

12-Step Programs

Adult Children of Alcoholics (ACA)
2225 Sepulveda Blvd. #200
Torrance, CA 90505
(213) 534-1815

Alcoholics Anonymous World Services, Inc.
P.O. Box 459
Grand Central Station
New York, NY 10163
(212) 686-1100

Co-dependents Anonymous (CODA)
P.O. Box 33577
Phoenix, AZ 85067
(602) 277-7991

Incest Survivors Anonymous (ISA)
P.O. Box 5613
Long Beach, CA 90805
(213) 428-5599

Parents Anonymous
6733 South Sepulveda Boulevard
Suite 270
Los Angeles, CA 90045
800-421-0353

National program of professionally facilitated self-help groups
to help parents who have abused their children or who are
afraid they will abuse them; 1,200 chapters nationwide.

Sex Addicts Anonymous
P.O. Box 300
Simi Valley, CA 93062
(805) 581-3343

Survivors of Incest Anonymous World Service Office
P.O. Box 21817
Baltimore, MD 21222
(301) 282-3400

Adult Children of Alcoholics (ACA), **Alcoholics Anonymous (AA)**, **Gamblers Anonymous (GA)**, **Incest Survivors Anonymous (ISA)**, **Narcotics Anonymous (NA)** and **Sex and Love Addicts Anonymous (SLAA)** are national organizations whose local chapters should be listed in your telephone directory. If you have trouble locating a group, call your local hospital, outpatient treatment center, community service agency, college counseling center, library or mental health agency.

Appendix II:
Recommended Reading

Spousal Abuse

Engel, Beverly. *The Emotionally Abused Woman.* New York: Fawcett Columbine, 1990.

Forward, Susan. *Men Who Hate Women and the Women Who Love Them.* New York: Bantam Books, 1986.

Martin, Del. *Battered Wives.* Rev. ed. San Francisco: Volcano Press, 1981.

Sonkin, Daniel, and Michael Durphy. *Learning to Live Without Violence: A Handbook for Men.* San Francisco: Volcano Press, 1985.

Walker, Lenore. *The Battered Woman.* New York: Harper & Row, 1979.

Sexual Compulsions and Addictions

Carnes, Patrick. *Out of the Shadows: Understanding Sexual Addiction.* Minneapolis: CompCare Publications, 1985.

_____. *Contrary to Love: Helping the Sexual Addict.* Minneapolis: CompCare Publications, 1988.

_____. *Don't Call It Love: Recovering from Sexual Addiction.* New York: Bantam, 1991.

Earle, Ralph, and Gregory Crow. *Lonely All the Time: Recognizing, Understanding and Overcoming Sexual Addiction for Addicts and Co-dependents.* New York: Simon and Schuster, 1989.

Money, J. *Vandalized Lovemaps.* Buffalo, N.Y.: Prometheus Books, 1990. A book about how paraphilias develop.

Mura, David. *A Male Grief: Notes on Pornography and Addiction.* Minneapolis: Milkweed Editions, 1987. Convincing thesis on the negative effects of using pornography. Milkweed Editions, P.O. Box 3226, Minneapolis, MN 55403.

Rape and Sexual Harassment

Levy, Barrie. *Dating Violence: Young Women in Danger.* Seattle, WA: Seal Press, 1991.

Parrot, Andrea. *Coping with Date Rape and Acquaintance Rape.* New York: Rosen Publishing Group, 1988. For adolescents and teens in recovery.

Childhood Sexual Abuse

Recovery

Bass, Ellen, and Laura Davis. *The Courage to Heal: A Guide for Women Survivors of Child Sexual Abuse.* New York: Harper & Row, 1988. Section on intimacy and sexuality.

Engel, Beverly. *The Right to Innocence: Healing the Trauma of Childhood Sexual Abuse.* New York: Ballantine, 1989.

Lew, Mike. *Victims No Longer: Men Recovering from Incest and Other Child Sexual Abuse.* New York: HarperCollins, 1990. General Information about sexual effects; helpful section on sexual orientation confusion.

Love, Patricia. *The Emotional Incest Syndrome: What to Do When a Parent's Love Rules Your Life.* New York: Bantam Books, 1990.

Sexual Recovery

Maltz, Wendy, and Beverly Holman. *Incest and Sexuality: A Guide to Understanding and Healing.* Lexington, Mass.: Lexington Books, 1987.

_____. *The Sexual Healing Journey: A Guide for Survivors of Sexual Abuse.* New York: HarperCollins Publishers, Inc., 1992.

General Information

Butler, Sandra. *Conspiracy of Silence: The Trauma of Incest.* Updated ed. San Francisco: Volcano Press, 1985.

Crewdson, John. *By Silence Betrayed: Sexual Abuse of Children in America.* Boston: Little, Brown, 1988.

Finkelhor, David. *Child Sexual Abuse: New Theory and Research.* New York: The Free Press, 1984.

Forward, Susan, and Craig Buck. *Betrayal of Innocence: Incest and Its Devastation.* Los Angeles: Jeremy P. Tarcher, Inc., 1978.

Herman, Judith. *Father-Daughter Incest.* Cambridge: Harvard University Press, 1981.

Masson, Jeffrey Moussaieff. *The Assault on Truth: Freud's Suppression of the Seduction Theory.* New York: Farrar, Straus & Giroux, 1984.

Rush, Florence. *The Best-Kept Secret: Sexual Abuse of Children*. Englewood Cliffs, N.J.: Prentice-Hall, 1980.

Russell, Diana. *The Secret Trauma: Incest in the Lives of Girls and Women*. New York: Basic Books, 1986.

Child Abuse

Farmer, Steven. *Adult Children of Abusive Parents: A Healing Program for Those Who Have Been Physically, Sexually or Emotionally Abused*. Los Angeles: Lowell House, 1989.

Gil, Eliana. *Outgrowing the Pain: A Book for and About Adults Abused as Children*. San Francisco: Launch Press, 1983.

Miller, Alice. *The Drama of the Gifted Child: The Search for the True Self*. New York: Basic Books, 1981.

_____. *For Your Own Good: Hidden Cruelty in Child-rearing and the Roots of Violence*. New York: Farrar, Straus & Giroux, 1984.

_____. *Thou Shalt Not Be Aware: Society's Betrayal of the Child*. New York: New American Library, 1986.

Your Body and Body Image

Chernin, Kim. *The Obsession: Reflections on the Tyranny of Slenderness*. New York: Harper & Row, 1981.

Hutchinson, Marcia Germaine. *Transforming Body Image*. New York: Crossing Press, 1985. Step-by-step exercises to help integrate your body, mind and self-image, and to begin to love and accept yourself just the way you are. Box 640, Trumansburg, NY 14886.

McFarland, Barbara, and Tyeis Baker-Baumann. *Shame and Body Image: Culture and the Compulsive Eater*. Deerfield Beach, Fla.: Health Communications, Inc., 1990.

Help for Partners
(of Survivors, Abusers, Sex Addicts)

Beattie, Melody. *Codependent No More.* San Francisco: Harper/Hazeldon, 1987.

_____. *Beyond Codependency.* San Francisco: Harper/Hazeldon, 1989.

Engel, Beverly. *Partners in Recovery: How Mates, Lovers & Other Prosurvivors Can Learn to Cope with Adult Survivors of Childhood Sexual Abuse.* New York: Fawcett Columbine, 1991.

McEnvoy, Alan, and Jeff Brookings. *If She Is Raped: A Book for Husbands, Fathers and Male Friends.* Holmes Beach, Fla.: Learning Publications, 1984. P.O. Box 1326, Holmes Beach, FL 33509.

Norwood, Robin. *Women Who Love Too Much: When You Keep Wishing and Hoping He'll Change.* Los Angeles: Jeremy P. Tarcher, Inc. 1985.

Schneider, Jennifer. *Back from Betrayal: Surviving His Affairs.* New York: Harper & Row, 1988.

Wegscheider-Cruse, Sharon. *Choice-Making: For Co-Dependents, Adult Children and Spirituality Seekers.* Pompano Beach, Fla.: Health Communications, Inc., 1985.

Bibliography

Berendzen, Richard. *Come Here.* New York: Villard Books, 1993.

Brinkley, Dannion. *Saved by the Light.* New York: Villard Books, 1994.

Campbell, Joseph. *The Portable Jung.* New York: Penguin Books, 1976.

Engel, Beverly. *The Emotionally Abused Woman.* New York: Fawcett Columbine, 1990.

Gibran, Kahlil. *The Prophet.* New York: Alfred Knopf, 1923.

Masterson, James F. *The Search for the Real Self: Unmasking the Personality Disorders of Our Age.* New York: The Free Press, 1988.

Middelton-Moz, Jane. *Shame and Guilt: Masters of Disguise.* Deerfield Beach, Fla.: Health Communications, Inc., 1990.

Miller, William. *Your Golden Shadow.* San Francisco: Harper & Row, 1989.

Moore, Thomas. *Care of the Soul: A Guide for Cultivating Depth and Sacredness in Everyday Life.* New York: HarperCollins, 1992.

Sinetar, Marsha. *Elegant Choices, Healing Choices: Finding Grace and Wholeness in Everything We Choose.* New York: Paulist Press, 1988.

Smedes, Lewis B. *Shame and Grace: Healing the Shame We Don't Deserve.* San Francisco: HarperSanFrancisco, 1993.

Walker, Brian Browne. *The I Ching or Book of Changes.* New York: St. Martin's Press, 1992.